DMU 0557168 01 6

Dep

Li

D

Ple
Fir

e

The Social Market Foundation

The Foundation's main activity is to commission and publish original papers by independent academic and other experts on key topics in the economic and social fields, with a view to stimulating public discussion on the performance of markets and the social framework within which they operate. The Foundation is a registered charity and a company limited by guarantee. It is independent of any political party or group and is financed by the sale of publications and by voluntary donations from individuals, organisations and companies. The views expressed in publications are those of the authors and do not represent a corporate opinion of the Foundation.

Chairman
David Lipsey (Lord Lipsey of Tooting Bec)

Members of the Board
Viscount Chandos
Gavyn Davies
David Edmonds
Brian Pomeroy
Shriti Vadera

Director
Ann Rossiter

D1147205

Kindly supported by Rainer

Rainer is the national charity for under-supported young people. Last year we worked with 18,000 young people and young adults across the country, providing and acting as a gateway to a full range of services for those caught up in the criminal justice system, in or leaving care or those who face challenges with education or employability. Our policy and communications work draws on this experience to raise awareness of the issues faced by under-supported young people and to inform public policy and practice. This year marks our 200th anniversary. www.raineronline.org

First published by
The Social Market Foundation,
September 2006

The Social Market Foundation
11 Tufton Street
London SW1P 3QB

Copyright © The Social Market
Foundation, 2006

The moral right of the authors has been
asserted. All rights reserved. Without
limiting the rights under copyright reserved
above, no part of this publication may be
reproduced, stored or introduced into a
retrieval system, or transmitted, in any form
or by any means (electronic, mechanical,
photocopying, recording, or otherwise),
without the prior written permission of both
the copyright owner and the publisher of
this book.

DE MONTFORT UNIVERSITY
LIBRARY:
....
B/code
....
Fund: 140 Date: 13/6/07
....
Sequence
....
Class: 364.63094
....
Suffix: RET

Contents

About the authors

Nick Aldridge, Director of Strategy and Communications, acevo

Nick Aldridge is acevo's Director of Strategy and Communications. He recently completed a secondment to the Cabinet Office, working on an action plan for increased third sector involvement in public service delivery and reform.

Nick is the author of "Communities in Control", published by the Social Market Foundation, and was a member of the steering group that developed the sector's new code of governance. He writes a column in *Social Enterprise Magazine*.

Stephen Bubb, Chief Executive, acevo

Stephen Bubb is Chief Executive of the Association of Chief Executives of Voluntary Organisations (acevo) where his work on leadership and sector funding has radically shifted attitudes and policies. Described by the *Financial Times* as a leading proponent of boardroom reform, Stephen is also known as an influential networker.

He is currently an Independent Assessor for government appointments, a Council member of the Public Management and Policy Association, and a fellow of the RSA. He is the Chair of the Strategy Committee of Guy's & St Thomas' NHS Foundation Trust. He is a member of the *Sunday Times*/YouGov Think Tank of the country's top strategic thinkers and influencers and a member of the Cabinet Office's Honours Advisory Committee. This year Stephen is to become Secretary General of a European Leaders Network, having steered its set up and has recently become Chair of the Adventure Capital Fund.

Julian Corner, Chief Executive, Revolving Doors Agency

Julian Corner became Revolving Doors Agency's Chief Executive in 2004. He previously worked as a civil servant in the Department of Education and Employment, the Cabinet Office, the Office of the Deputy Prime Minister and finally the Home Office. He was lead author of the Social Exclusion Unit's report 'Reducing Re-offending by Ex-prisoners' and coordinated the Home Office's 'National Reducing Re-offending Action Plan'.

Julian contributes to a number of Government advisory groups and currently acts as a trustee of Housing Association Charitable Trust.

Stuart Etherington, Chief Executive, NCVO

Stuart Etherington was appointed Chief Executive of NCVO in 1994. Previously he was Chief Executive of the Royal National Institute for Deaf People. He has been awarded an honorary doctorate from Brunel University and is a Visiting Professor in voluntary sector policy at South Bank University. Stuart is a trustee of Business in the Community, CIVICUS Global and the Experience Corps.

His government appointments include the Economic and Social Research Council and the Prime Minister's Delivery Unit. He has also served on the Cabinet Office Performance and Innovation Unit's Advisory Board on the voluntary sector and the Treasury's Cross Cutting Review on the role of the voluntary sector.

Harry Fletcher, Assistant General Secretary,
National Association of Prison Officers (Napo)

For over 20 years Harry has had responsibility for press, parliamentary activity, public speaking and campaigning at Napo, and previously at the National Council for Civil Liberties. He edits and writes Napo News, which is a monthly magazine for all union members.

In 2004 he established the first all-party trade union group on criminal justice issues. This was followed in 2006 by the establishment of a similar cross-party group for the family courts.

He has written regularly for various magazines, has

presented papers at national conferences on a range of issues including public protection, drug testing and the Family Courts. He has also spoken at fringe meetings at the TUC and all main political party conferences.

Nicola Lowit, Deputy Director, Commissioning and Contestability Programme, NOMS

Nicola Lowit is Deputy Director of the Commissioning and Contestability Programme, and led the project team which put in place the first stage of commissioning across NOMS in April 2006.

Nicola has a background in education and training, and worked in the voluntary, public and independent sectors before joining the Prison Service in 1999, first as an Education Advisor, then in the Juvenile Group where she was responsible for negotiating and managing the service level agreement with the Youth Justice Board for the delivery of custodial places for juveniles.

Professor Rod Morgan, Chair, Youth Justice Board

Rod Morgan became Chair of the Youth Justice Board in April 2004. He was formerly HM Chief Inspector of Probation for England and Wales. Before that he was Professor of Criminal Justice in the faculty of law at the University of Bristol, where he remains Professor Emeritus.

Rod has served as an expert advisor to the Council of Europe and Amnesty International on custodial conditions and process, and the prevention of torture – a topic on which he has written several books, including the Council of Europe's own guide to the Work of the European Committee for the Prevention of Torture.

He is the co-editor of the principal text in the field of criminology in the UK, *The Oxford Handbook of Criminology* and is currently preparing a similar text on probation policy, research and practice.

Joyce Moseley, Chief Executive, Rainer

Joyce Moseley has been Rainer's chief executive since October 1999.

She served two terms of office as a member of the Youth

Justice Board from its formation in 1998 and was formerly a director of social services and vice president of the association of directors of social services.

Joyce is a trustee of 'The Who Cares? Trust', which promotes the needs of children in public care, and of an inner London community regeneration trust.

Natalie Tarry, Director of Research, Social Market Foundation

Natalie Tarry is Director of Research at the Social Market Foundation and is responsible for SMF's research programme. The programme includes work streams on public service reform, the operation of markets, life chances and the public realm.

Before joining the SMF, Natalie spent fours years working for the New Local Government Network, an independent local government think tank, where she worked and published on user choice, city regions, PPPs, regeneration and governance issues.

Prior to that Natalie worked at the European Parliament in Brussels and for a research institute/consultancy in Frankfurt.

Foreword

The third sector has played a large role in the rapid and effective development of public services. Through an amalgamation of community organisations, social enterprises and co-operatives, the Government has ensured that vital services are delivered to the maximum standard whilst preserving important parts of the public sector ethos. Public services across the board - from hospitals and prisons to the transport infrastructure - are being transformed by the third sector in the UK.

Next to embrace this tidal wave of change should be the National Offender Management Service (NOMS). We need a diverse range of interventions for the diverse range of people we aim to serve. This is not to say that the prison service has not progressed considerably so far. Since 1997 spending on prisons has increased by over 30% in real terms and spending on probation has increased by 70%. NOMS spends over £800 million a year, a quarter of its budget on private and non-profit providers, in developing new prisons or for use in prison escort services a well as electronic monitoring services. This has been successful, with these new prisons improving each year.

The competitive market in the prison estate has been beneficial to the Prison Service. Private prisons have become a significant and effective part of the estate, raising standards of delivery, increasing capacity, and introducing dynamic management practices into the system. The National Probation Service has delivered real improvements too – using group work programmes to achieve record level performance. Community penalty enforcement rates, for example, have risen from 43% in 2001 to over 90% now.

However, it is important to recognise that Government or the market cannot always offer the best solution to problems within the custodial sector. We need reform to help us meet targets to reduce the rate of reoffending by 5% by 2008 and by 10% by 2010, for example. I would also like to see greater consistency in performance in the service across organisational and geographical boundaries.

We have an opportunity to embrace change and use the competition of the third sector to drive up standards. I want to see a debate about what role the third sector can play in providing services for probation. The third sector could offer a great deal to probation services. We must give such organisations a chance to provide services that have been locked in the hands of those who have not always delivered to the needs of individual communities.

Patrick Carter's review of the correctional services in England and Wales, "Managing Offenders, Reducing Crime", concluded that improved effectiveness and value for money would be delivered through greater competition from private and voluntary providers and through establishing a purchaser/provider split to give public value partnership. We can challenge existing suppliers to demonstrate that they continue to offer the best value for money to the taxpayer and, if they do not, offer other providers the opportunity to do it better instead. A history of the custodial sector shows that the introduction of contestability drives up performance on the part, not only of the new providers who enter the market, but also of the remaining public sector providers who raise their game to meet the challenge.

What we envisage is a phased programme whereby certain elements of probation activity are market-tested to find the best provider. In some cases, that provider will come from the voluntary and community sector or private. But in many cases, we expect that the best provider will continue to be the public sector, either because the public sector is already delivering a high-quality service in the particular case and/or because the competition has provided an incentive to raise performance further. We will be looking at how we can encourage the voluntary and community sector to compete for contracts either bidding directly or in partnership with trusts and other providers.

The third sector has valuable experience in social enterprise and indeed social justice. It has the knowledge and the guidance to meet specific personal needs and it can tackle newly arising social issues that probation is closely associated with. With its experience and independence to innovate, it has a unique ability to be flexible and offer joined up service delivery. We should debate how to use this to improve our service – working across organisational boundaries to reduce re-offending and increase public confidence. This collection of essays opens an important debate that should help to revolutionise how probation operates.

Gerry Sutcliffe MP
Under-Secretary of State for Criminal Justice
and Offender Management

Introduction and Executive Summary

1 Prison Reform Trust, *Bromley Briefings Prison File* (London: Prison Reform Trust, 2006).

2 CBI, Transforming Criminal Justice: Protecting the public – Partnership in offender management (London: CBI, 2006).

3 Social Exclusion Unit, *Reducing Re-offending by Ex-prisoners* (West Yorkshire: Social Exclusion, 2002).

4 Erwin James, 'Insider looking out', *The Guardian*, 5 April 2006.

5 Patrick Carter, *Managing Offenders, Reducing Crime* (London: Home Office, 2003).

Background to the probation service reforms

Since 1997 spending on prisons has risen by more than 25% in real terms since 2001, while spending on probation has risen by 39% over the same period.[1] Despite major new investment, almost 60% of people who pass through the criminal justice system re-offend within two years.[2] Drastic action is needed to combat this cycle of re-offending; with estimated costs near 11 billion pounds per year.[3]

High-profile cases such as the murder of investment banker John Monkton committed under probation supervision have added to the pressure for rapid improvements and have led to an attempt at "rebalancing the criminal justice system in favour of the law-abiding majority and the victim", something that some commentators have cautioned against as a move towards greater retribution rather than rehabilitation.[4]

An independent review of correctional services produced by Carter in December 2003 also came to the conclusion that the current probation system was failing and that a new approach was needed.[5]

In particular, the report recommended:
- tough and rigorous sentences for offenders
- a new role for the judiciary
- end-to-end offender management
- improving contestability and competition within the corrections market.

The Home Office responded with the publication of 'Reducing

Crime – Changing Lives' aimed at delivering these improvements, which proposed the introduction of market competition and contestability in to the probation service.[6] It set out proposals to manage offenders under an integrated National Offender Management Service (NOMS) that would focus on end-to-end management of offenders.

6 David Blunkett, *Reducing Crime, Changing Lives* (London: Home Office, 2004).

Is contestability the solution?

Contestability is central to the government's reform programme. Previously, a network of local Probation Boards comprised the National Probation Service (NPS). Probation Boards had the statutory right to provide all probation services. From April 2006, the NPS was transformed into a purchaser-provider model with the National Offender Management Service (NOMS) commissioning providers from the public, voluntary and private sectors. Probation Boards will become Trusts, working with their Regional Offender Manager (ROMs).

As the Home Office website states: "As a commissioning organisation, NOMS' activities will be carried out by a range of providers, primarily those within the National Probation Service and HM Prison Service. NOMS will use commissioning from a range of providers to secure places in custody or on community sentences, based on quality, value for money and innovation. It will use providers in the public, commercial and not-for-profit/voluntary sector."

In effect, the NPS now acts as a purchasing agency, employing market mechanisms to identify the best, most cost effective source of service delivery. For the first phase of this process, a target was set of five percent of the main resource grant to be contracted out to the voluntary community and private sectors, by the second half of the current financial year. This target builds on a longstanding partnership with the voluntary sector. Over a thousand different voluntary and community sector organisations are working in the prison and probation area, including drug treatment, resettlement and welfare to work programmes.

In accordance with sweeping public service reforms, greater third sector participation in public service delivery is deemed key to providing innovative, value for money services. In a speech to the Future Services Network's Three Sectors confer-

7 Tony Blair, *Voluntary Sector Speech at the Future Services Network Conference*, 22 June 2006.

8 Helen Edwards, *Message from Helen Edwards: review of the Criminal Justice System*, 20 July 2006.

ence in June 2006, Prime Minster Tony Blair said:

"… if we want to increase the amount of creativity and innovation then we should be using the creativity and innovation there is in whatever part of society. And the truth is some of those organisations that are doing the most ground-breaking…, most innovative work are to be found in the voluntary sector today."[7]

In a recent statement Helen Edwards, the Chief Executive of NOMS, echoed these sentiments:

"We want to get a wider range of partners involved in managing offenders and cutting re-offending. Therefore, we will legislate to open up probation to other providers, and will only award contracts to those who can prove they will deliver reductions in re-offending, and keep the public safe. We need to bring in expertise from the private and voluntary sectors to drive up the quality and performance of community punishments."[8]

The proposals have come under fierce criticism and have provoked an intense ideological debate as Nicola Lowit from NOMS describes in Chapter 1. She makes the case for commissioning and contestability and explains the government's rationale for the reform program. She views the introduction of competition as a key driver to deliver service improvements in the prison and probation service.

Those opposed have seen them as little more than the 'first steps' along the road to privatisation. Almost entirely ignored in the debate is the positive and sustainable role the third sector might play in the reform process, unencumbered by the profit motives of the private sector.

Joyce Moseley, the Chief Executive of Rainer, points out in her contribution that the contestability agenda is, first and foremost, a mechanism that ensures that all sectors have an opportunity to contribute to service delivery. Currently only three per cent of the budget for adult offenders is spent outside the probation service. She further emphasises that suggesting that the third sector might be better at delivering services is not to make an ideological argument. Nor does it threaten the raison d'être of public provision as is often alleged. Instead she argues that genuine contestability would lead to better and more innovative approaches developing across the three sectors.

Julian Corner takes a different view and sees a replacement of the public delivery model simply with VCO providers as essentially delivering the same services by different providers. More importantly, he fears this may lead voluntary and community organsations to lose their unique perspectives and undermine their ability to challenge those who commission services because they are afraid of losing out on contracts and funding.

The third sector in probation

The third sector has a long history of providing user-focussed support and services to disadvantaged client groups and has the ability to engage with those often considered hardest to reach. In their contribution, Nick Aldridge and Stephen Bubb highlight successful examples of voluntary sector involvement in the probation service, such as Rathbone's "Prove it" programme.

VCOs' role in the criminal justice system is not new, as Joyce Moseley reminds us in Chapter 2. It has often been particularly marginalised, excluded and vulnerable groups, such as offenders, that VCOs volunteers have built relationships with. These relationships tend to be characterised by trust, continuity, ongoing engagement and hope, and are often unique to the sector's approach, as highlighted by Rod Morgan, Chair of the Youth Justice Board. A new role for VCOs may challenge some of these relationships.

This publication gives a voice to a range of commentators from the third sector, academia, government and others operating in the criminal justice system. Their contributions highlight several reasons why prisons and probation services might benefit from volunteers and partnerships with the voluntary sector, including:

- VCOs are able to reach groups and individuals that other organisations often find hard to reach, such as young people, offenders from a black or ethnic minority background, drug users and offenders with mental health problems etc.
- VCOs tend to provide flexible, personalised and tailored services, as they are developed from the bottom up to respond to the needs of those using their services and are therefore particularly responsive.

9 Patricia Hewitt, *Patient choice – the key to NHS future,* 14 June 2006.

10 Further detail can be found in a previous SMF publication on the voluntary sector by Nick Aldridge, *Communities in Control: The new third sector agenda for public service reform* (London: SMF, 2005).

- For prisoners, the fact that a volunteer chooses to spend time in a prison and is not a paid professional enhances his/her credibility. Trust is crucial in building positive relationships with prisoners, in particular with volunteer mentors, and thus is an important step in breaking the cycle of re-offending.
- This closeness to offenders makes many VCOs particularly suited to get involved in the debate about future service design and improved solutions.
- VCOs are diverse and reflect their clientele which means that they may be better suited to deliver probation services than monolithic public services.

The report also explores how the reform and improvement agenda, involving an increased role for the third sector, could be taken forward. This includes an assessment of the current barriers and challenges to reform, particularly around procurement capacity, commissioning and a level playing field.

Barriers and challenges

Despite the potential benefits for all parties concerned, there are significant barriers to greater voluntary and community sector (VCS) involvement. These barriers are of course not unique to the probation service. Health Secretary Patricia Hewitt's speech to the King's Fund conference in June 2006 noted some of the broader difficulties:

"Key messages emerging from the Third Sector Commissioning Taskforce include the notion that Commissioners need more clearly to understand the third sector, the organisations within it and their contribution to the commissioning process, both to inform service design, and as potential providers. In addition the taskforce has posed some challenges about how the mindset of commissioning needs to change."[9]

Stephen Bubb and Nick Aldridge look at some of the barriers to greater VCOs involvement in more detail in Chapter 4.[10] Many of these were identified in the Treasury's Cross Cutting Review of 2002. Some progress is expected in the forthcoming Action Plan, including:

- uncertainty of contract length

- funding the full costs of a service
- longer-term funding
- fairer risk sharing
- appropriate monitoring and accountability
- a level playing field
- perceived lack of professionalism.

However, systemic and attitudinal barriers to greater third sector involvement are not the only ones that VCOs need to overcome. There are some serious challenges for commissioners and for VCOs themselves in the NOMS agenda.

The commissioner/provider split that has driven improvements in the community care sector could also bring genuine benefits to those caught up in the criminal justice system and to the wider public. However, the design of the commissioning structures is vital for success and several of the reports' commentators point to potential problems. To be able to meet statutory contracts and monitoring and reporting targets, VCOs might have to replace some of their volunteers with more professional staff, therefore distancing themselves from their usual way of working and the offenders they work with. This might apply particularly to small, flexible VCOs trying to compete for large contracts.

Prescriptive contracts may undermine the value that VCOs can bring to the delivery of probation services. A focus on processes and systems, rather than outcomes would suppress innovation and flexibility and undermine attempts to achieve better services for offenders and reduce re-offending. Commissioners need to understand the differences between the sectors to enable the VCOs to flourish in this environment and operate in a level playing field.

A greater focus on commissioning might also lead to a challenge to VCOs' traditional values and objectives and to a less offender-focussed approach. As Stuart Etherington points out in Chapter 3, some contracts might require volunteers and staff to make recommendations that might potentially affect the liberty of an individual. This might not only challenge the individual organisation's ethics and that of its members, but also has the potential to undermine confidence and trust in the sector. This is a problem that Julian Corner also addresses in Chapter 5.

Some of the contributors regard the focus on contestability and competition as misplaced and unlikely to deliver a better probation service. They criticise the NOMS reforms for centralising the service and focusing on cost cutting and efficiency. Rod Morgan highlights the lessons from the successful youth justice delivery model which is based on local ownership and devolved decision-making. He challenges whether VCOs are better placed to deliver probation services than the public sector. He criticises NOMS for lacking local sensitivity and accountability. In Chapter 8, Harry Fletcher from the National Association of Prison Officers (Napo), the trade union for probation service staff outlines another alternative to the reforms based on the more localised, partnership-based Scottish system. He regards the current NOMS vision as a route to privatisation and prefers a model based on partnerships between the three sectors, rather than commissioning and contestability.

Conclusions

For contributors who see VCOs contributing positively to future probation service delivery, reform cannot be about simply exchanging one service provider for another. Instead success is dependent on service transformation and the added value that some VCOs might be able to deliver. Stuart Etherington from NCVO makes this case very compellingly in Chapter 3.

There is no consensus as to whether contestability in itself will be able to deliver the much-needed reduction in re-offending. Most contributors agree that allowing maximum flexibility for VCOs within the new framework is vital if innovations are to be fostered and successful relationships with offenders maintained.

Many of the views represented here are in line with the recommendations made in the government's Cross Cutting Review on longer-term funding streams which can allow VCOs to develop and grow and which lead to fairer risk sharing. There are a number of others it is worth highlighting:

For VCOs
- VCOs need to consider whether a contract interferes with their values, independence, mission and objectives before entering into partnerships or delivery agreements.

- VCOs need to continue to focus on advocacy and giving support, advice and information to offenders. Service delivery is only a part of their multi-faceted role.
- VCOs need to continue to work with volunteers to maintain the relationships and levels of trust which can develop between VCOs and offenders.
- Their proximity to offenders needs to be reflected in a greater role as service shapers and designers using evidence of what works from their delivery experience and insights gained through consultation.
- VCOs need to be realistic about what they can deliver. They need to be self-critical about their capacity and their approach. Many small charities are able to deliver excellent services to a particular niche of the community, but they might not be able to replicate these successes on a larger scale without becoming unduly dependent on government funding to sustain their growth/new size.

For NOMS

- Commissioners need to have a better understanding of the added value that VCOs can bring to the negotiating table and service delivery.
- A level playing field needs to exist that allows third sector organisations to genuinely compete for service delivery contracts in probation services.
- Commissioning must not exclude the many small, flexible and locally based organisations that can add particular value in favour of larger VCOs.
- NOMS must avoid using short-term contracts that lead to instability and funding insecurity and prevent VCOs from planning and developing efficient services.
- There needs to be a greater focus on outcomes not processes to leave room for innovation and local experimentation.
- A more localised or federalised delivery model might overcome some of the fears of over-bureaucratisation and potential distancing from traditional clientele.

Much of the Social Market Foundation's work emphasises the need for a healthy and strong public service culture in the UK within a context of competition, diversity of provision and a

11 Nick Aldridge (2005).

level playing field. A stronger role for VCOs is something previous SMF publications have highlighted.[11] Splitting up the commissioner and provider roles has driven improvements in other public service areas, but a mixed market and commissioning in NOMS is only a means to an end and not the end in itself. It serves the sole purpose of cutting re-offending and improving the probation service.

Government is trying to achieve two important aims: reducing the recidivism of offenders and restoring the public's trust in the service, while delivering value for the taxpayer. Too strong a focus on the second goal might result in a failure to bring about the drastically needed service improvements and a greater role for VCOs in helping to deliver the reduction in re-offending.

The emphasis on commissioning and contestability will only truly herald benefits and produce innovation if the voluntary sector is able to focus on holistic outcomes and operate across silos. If VCO partnerships and contracts are rigid and too prescriptive and only ape existing public sector provision, little improvement to re-offending will be delivered and the voluntary sector will continue to play a marginal role.

We hope that this publication will take the debate on probation reform forward and beyond the highly charged public vs. private provision argument that so often dominates the public service reform agenda. Otherwise we are in danger of ignoring a sector that has much to offer – a sector that founded the probation service and that is so often left out in the cold.

Natalie Tarry
Director of Research
Social Market Foundation

Chapter 1: The National Offender Management Service – the case for change

By Nicola Lowit

Crime is going down. But over half of all crimes are committed by people who have already been through the criminal justice system. And around 60% of people who have been through the system re-offend within two years. The National Offender Management Service spends over £3.3 billion on adult offender services each year, but there is a clear need to look at how these resources are invested to better protect the public and reduce re-offending.

The publication of the Carter Report in December 2003 and the subsequent announcement of the creation of a National Offender Management Service (NOMS) in early 2004 set down a marker for a radical and fundamental shift in the organisation and management of the prison and probation services in England and Wales.[12] The Home Office response to Carter *Reducing Crime, Changing Lives* set out the government's proposals for the creation of NOMS. In the foreword to the Home Office report, the then Home Secretary explicitly positioned these reforms as part of the government's wider public service reform agenda, and identified a 'once in a generation opportunity to reduce crime'.[13]

The case for the restructuring of prison and probation services in England and Wales has not gone away. The rise in caseloads of both services is increasing despite recorded crime rates falling.[14] The services are expensive to run, while signifi-

12 Patrick Carter (2003).

13 David Blunkett (2004).

14 The measurement of crime is notoriously difficult and I do not intend here to discuss the difficulties, suffice to say it is generally accepted that recorded crime is only a small fraction of crimes committed.

15 Since 1997, spending on prisons has risen by more than 30% in real terms, and spending on probation has risen by over 70%.

16 During a performance test, public sector prisons were given six months to produce a comprehensive performance improvement plan, followed by an evaluation of the plan which would lead to either a service level agreement being awarded to the public sector prison, or market testing with the public sector disbarred from bidding.

17 The report of an unannounced follow up inspection of Dartmoor Prison in 2006 "describes a prison that has been transformed" (HMIP 2006).

cant additional investment has only really enabled them to manage the increased workload.[15] Recently there have been some serious public protection failures, and re-offending rates remain staggeringly high. Not only that, but the investment climate has changed. The chance of substantial additional funding for resource-hungry criminal justice agencies on an ongoing basis appears remote.

As can be seen therefore, putting more and more money into existing organisational structures and systems will not be the means of delivering the step change in public protection and reducing re-offending, which is so urgently required. New structures are needed, which put the offender at the heart of the system, making a reality of end to end offender management, rather than structures based around existing ways of working. And new and innovative service delivery activity is needed, joining up custody and the community, as are better ways of prioritising increasingly scarce resources to better protect the public and reduce re-offending

NOMS was created with an explicit remit to introduce commissioning and contestability, as one of the three major planks of reform, the other two being rebalancing sentencing and end to end offender management. Lord Carter was explicit in his report about the benefits of competition, within the new structure, whereby public, private and voluntary sector providers compete to deliver more effective and efficient services.

Contestability, and the view that increased competition will help to drive performance improvement, is a key theme throughout the NOMS reforms. The evidence from the performance testing process within the prison service has shown that the challenge of contestability, in particular the option of contracting out underperforming prisons has been a catalyst for significantly improved performance, new ways of working and better value for money.[16] There have been some startling examples of change – Dartmoor being a prime example.[17]

In addition to increasing contestability – allowing private and voluntary sector providers to compete alongside the public sector for the delivery of both custodial and community penalties, NOMS is implementing commissioning. Commissioning describes a set of activities which are separate from actually running the services. These include identifying services needed;

specifying the service; negotiating funding and outcomes with the provider; monitoring performance; and accounting for what is being delivered. Regional commissioners are responsible for purchasing most adult offender services within their regions, and are accountable for delivery. Service providers no longer determine the services to be delivered, but deliver those services which have been purchased by the commissioner. Their accountability, as set out in "Reducing Crime, Changing Lives" is for the efficient operation of the services provided.[18]

Of course neither commissioning nor contestability is entirely new across NOMS. The Youth Justice reforms that came out of the Audit Commission report 'Misspent Youth', published in 1996, were an obvious precursor.[19] The Audit Commission found significant wasted resources, and described the system as uncoordinated, inefficient and ineffective. The resulting reforms split the purchasing from the provision of custodial places, with the Youth Justice Board (a non-departmental public body established in the 1998 Crime and Disorder Act) purchasing custodial places from the Prison Service as well as from private sector and local authority providers. New, multi-agency Youth Offender Teams were set up within every local authority to coordinate youth justice provision in their area and deliver a range of services and programmes to young offenders designed to reduce offending, many commissioned from other organisations. The Youth Justice Board, as well as acting as purchaser of custodial places, is responsible for setting targets and monitoring performance across the youth justice system.

The prison service has not been exempt from major structural changes arising from the public sector reform agenda either. As well as organisational changes, such as the change to Agency status in 1993, and the contracting out of services such as education and escorts to private providers, the benefits of internal competition have been emphasised through such measures as the weighted scorecard, market testing and performance testing. In addition, around 8% of prisoners in England and Wales are held in private prisons, this includes private sector management of publicly built prisons, as well as the prisons built and run by private companies under the Private Finance Initiative.[20]

Commissioning and contestability provoke heated ideolog-

18 David Blunkett (2004).

19 Audit Commission, *Misspent Youth: Young people and crime* (Yorkshire: Audit Commission Publications, 1996).

20 S. Nathan, *Prison Privatisation in the United Kingdom,* in Coyle, Campbell and Neufield (eds.) *Capitalist Punishment: prison privatisation and human rights* (Zed Books), p. 165.

21 Mick Ryan, *Privatisation, corporate interest and the future shape and ethos of the prison service,* in *Privatisation and Market Testing in the Prison Service* (London: Prison Reform Trust, 1994), p.17.

ical debate particularly around the issue of the "privatisation" of corrections; the morality or otherwise of profiting from punishment. However, the reality is that even before the introduction of competition, private interests have always profited from corrections, whether it was construction companies involved in building or refurbishing prisons, or companies providing services to prisoners. Once this is acknowledged, the debate then becomes "not so much a crude struggle between the public and the private, but rather a debate about exactly where, and on what terms, private interests should be involved".[21] The voluntary sector has been involved for much longer than the state in the delivery of offender services; the modern probation service has its roots in charity. So the argument becomes a pragmatic one – does it work?, rather than a moral issue – is it right?

Whatever one's views, private and voluntary sector involvement in the delivery of correctional services is bound to raise questions around accountability and legitimacy, in particular around the moral legitimacy of the state devolving the administration and delivery of punishment. However, the argument is not nearly as simple as the public/private dichotomy might suggest. Not only has the voluntary sector always had a significant role in delivering public services across the board, but questions such as who is accountable, how is penal policy developed, who has an interest in the expansion or contraction of the custodial sector, as well as arguments about the legitimacy of prison regimes, are equally valid whether services are delivered by the public, private or voluntary sectors. Within a commissioning system, private and voluntary sector providers are clearly accountable to the state through the contractual mechanisms; indeed, it can be argued that there is significantly greater accountability through rigorous contract management and auditing arrangements than through the state providing services directly.

So we know that neither commissioning nor contestability is new across NOMS, and we know that they constitute a major strand of the NOMS reform programme. But the question remains; why go down this particular route, rather than, say, stronger line management to improve performance, or giving grants to voluntary sector organisations who work with offenders?

Why commissioning? Because as previously outlined, new systems are needed which put the offender at the heart of what we do, rather than systems which suit existing organisational structures and ways of working. NOMS needs to bring in the best possible people and organisations to work with every offender. This means moving away from decisions about services being based largely on what has been provided before, or on organisational capacity. Instead decisions should be made based on the need to protect the public and turn offenders away from crime. Separating out decisions about what needs to be provided from those who provide services, allows for responsive and effective public service provision. This is what commissioning is about.

So commissioning is the vehicle through which NOMS will achieve its goals relating to public protection and reducing re-offending. It is the key mechanism through which NOMS will protect the public and punish offenders whilst at the same time tackling the linked factors that make them more likely to commit crime again. Of course no single agency can do this alone, and it requires close joint working with a wide range of partners beyond the criminal justice system. Around half of public funding on adult offenders comes from other government departments. Regional commissioners are key to developing the links with other agencies, partners and stakeholders and the regional reducing re-offending boards have a vital part to play. NOMS is also working with a number of partners, and has developed three strong alliances – the Corporate Alliance, the Civic Society Alliance, and the Faith and Voluntary Sector Alliance – to promote and encourage greater involvement from employers, local authorities, and voluntary and faith organisations in reducing re-offending.

Moving to commissioning helps NOMS to:
- think and plan more strategically and proactively, less short-term and reactively
- think about the services required, not focus on what we have had historically
- plan development on the basis of the properly assessed needs of offenders in each area
- set policy not in terms of detailed process, but in terms of the

22 Home Office, *Improving Prison and Probation Services: public value partnerships* (London: Home Office, 2006).

outcomes we want to see
- free up providers to manage their businesses and to generate more innovative approaches and solutions than would be the case if we try to run it all from Whitehall
- allow providers to focus on a clear, longer term statement of what we want, with greater "policy stability"
- ensure policy development is planned, coherent and funded
- drive up the quality of service and make it more consistent across the country
- drive out unnecessary cost and improve productivity, for re-investment in better services
- allow scope for variation in approach and in priorities regionally and locally, rather than 'one size fits all' across the nation.

Alongside commissioning, NOMS is extending contestability as a lever to drive performance improvements across all providers. The publication in August 2006 of *Improving prison and probation services: public value partnerships* set out NOMS' strategic intentions for contestability, and the initial programme of competition.[22]

So why contestability? As discussed above, there is evidence that competition, and a contestable environment, has contributed to standards being driven up in the custodial sector. But this is not about creating competing services for the sake of competition, and this is certainly not about privatising public services. This is not an ideological position, but a pragmatic one. NOMS wants the best possible providers delivering the most effective services so that the public are protected and crime is reduced.

The expectation is that there will be a thriving mixed economy of public, private and voluntary sector providers, and a wide range of partnerships and consortia in operation. Initially it is likely that the public sector will lead most partnerships, but this may not be the case in future, although the public sector will almost certainly retain a very significant role in the delivery of NOMS services. A range of approaches to increasing partnership working and driving service improvements are included, and the programme includes a major extension of sub-contracting. The voluntary sector already delivers through contracts and sub-contracts, NOMS works with something over a thousand different organisations already. And the voluntary sector will continue to make a significant contribution to the delivery of NOMS' objectives. The work of all providers, whether from the public, private or voluntary sectors will be better co-ordinated and focused on the key objectives of public protection and reducing re-offending. If any provider fails to deliver, the commissioners will have the option of choosing another provider to deliver the service unless performance quickly improves.

The National Offender Management Service represents one of the most ambitious change programmes across government. Resources are tight and caseloads are increasing. New and innovative ways of prioritising scarce resources into areas where we are likely to see the most benefits in terms of protecting the public and reducing re-offending are needed. The voluntary sector has a proud history in social policy, and an increasing role to play in the delivery of offender services. Commissioning and contestability will enable that to happen.

The modern probation service has its roots in charity.

Chapter 2: Throwing away the key? The historical and modern context of charities working in the criminal justice system

By Joyce Moseley

You only have to scan through the chapters in this book to see the diversity of opinion within and around the voluntary sector. Some commentators even question whether you can describe the 170,000 general charities and up to 350,000 community groups as a unified sector at all – let alone agree on a name (third sector, charity, non-profit and so on). Yet Voluntary and Community Organisations (VCOs) have come to play an increasingly central role in social policy, both in the UK and across the globe.

Indeed, the reforms introduced within public services in the 1980s and the hugely influential Deakin Commission have seen the contribution of the sector grow enormously, while across the Atlantic, a form of 'third party government' has had a similar impact. Both the speed and the size of the reforms have focused unprecedented attention on VCOs with little debate about the associated opportunities and consequences. Most recently this debate has focused on the criminal justice system, fuelled by the planned changes under the National Offender Management Service. What role can VCOs play? What are the implications and risks? What policies do we need to put in place? And do 'charities' have any role in delivering justice and dealing with offenders anyway?

Let's take that last question first, as it's possibly the simplest to address. As with many other areas of social policy, including housing, social care or health, voluntary organisations' contribution often pre-dates the state's involvement. Next year sees the centenary of the probation service. But this modern, public agency has charity at its roots – and began with a single donation:

"Offence after offence and sentence after sentence appear to be the inevitable lot of him whose foot has once slipped. Can nothing be done to arrest the downward career?"

So wrote Frederick Rainer, a printer, in a letter to the Church of England Temperance Society (1876) along with a gift of five shillings. This donation initially paid for a single missionary at Southwark court. By 1880, eight full time missionaries were working in the metropolitan courts, increasing to 70 by 1894. The approach was a success and soon had the backing of police and magistrates. The London Police Court Mission as it became known broadened its work across the capital and beyond. Even the act of parliament which created the modern probation service in 1907 still left the bulk of the work with the mission and it was 1939 before it was truly nationalised, with a network of homes for young offenders, employment projects and other schemes continuing as a charitable operation under the name Rainer. Today, Frederick Rainer's legacy lives on in two national organisations – one public, one voluntary and while only one still bears his name we should not forget the shared origin.

The second branch of Rainer's history is the Philanthropic Society. This aimed to be the first organisation to tackle crime 'through prevention rather than punishment'. Along with groups like the Marine Society and Coram Family it set to work in 18th century England providing housing, education and employment opportunities to those involved, or at risk of involvement in crime. The observation from an early annual report that the approach is:

"one of economy – as well as benevolence – the Offender's Reformation being in every sense a far cheaper process than His repeated Detection, Trial and Punishment"

still holds true today, though it is perhaps too swiftly forgotten under political and media pressure to appear tough on crime, and with a spiralling prison population.

As with the early hospitals, or Octavia Hill's work on housing, the demarcations between sectors are not, and never have been, wide or permanent. Many of the success stories of the modern welfare state have the voluntary sector at their core and there has long been an inter-dependence between the state and charities. The question is not *can* charities run criminal justice services but *should* they, and if so under what conditions?

Contracting and 'devoluntarisation'

Advocates of the proposed National Offender Management Service (NOMS) argue that the intention is to improve the chances of reformation and reducing re-offending as stated above. It could be seen as natural that VCOs, who have been doing this work for centuries, get involved. However, there are some potential concerns about the structure of such involvement in public services, and some particular issues within the criminal justice system.

VCOs are rightly praised for the strengths that they can bring to this sort of work – their flexibility, focus on the needs of the end user and the trust that this inspires with clients. Arguably, they are able to reach groups or individuals that other agencies can't. But we need to be careful not to conflate claims about individual VCOs with claims about a whole sector. While there are numerous examples of innovation by charities, there are similarly innovative examples in other sectors. And the best local probation services will have strong links with those they work with – if they didn't they simply wouldn't be able to do their job.

Ideally, what NOMS presents (as did community care reforms before it) is a mechanism to ensure the best approaches from across the sectors are taken up. The argument is not that voluntary providers could do a better job simply because of their voluntary status, it is that currently we do not know and are not given the opportunity to try – just three per cent of probation service's budgets for adult offenders is spent outside the probation service. The small number of voluntary projects that are working are often doing so against a background of short-term funding and a lack of influence over the wider approach.

The commissioner-provider split is one that has driven improvements in the community care sector and could bring genuine benefits to those caught up in the criminal justice system and to the wider public. It also gives voluntary agencies a clear platform on which to show their strengths and prove that their approaches can work. Across the fields of mental health, drug and alcohol treatment and even healthcare, voluntary agencies have dramatically increased their role through 'contracting out' and NOMS could signify a similar future for criminal justice. There are, of course, a number of different structures that can realise this approach and it's vital that commissioning and market structures are designed in such a way to improve services and enable providers to deliver to their strengths. And this is an area in which further concerns have been raised.

If the best voluntary agencies really are able to innovate, provide needs-based services and inspire trust in those they work with, some fear that these characteristics will be lost under burdensome statutory contracts. Agencies may become more bureaucratic in order to meet reporting and monitoring requirements, while volunteers may be replaced with professional staff and the sheer growth in size may move the organisation further from its client base. The very characteristics which appeal about voluntary agencies are lost in giving them that role. Or so the argument goes.

Academic research has indeed found that the expansion of community care contracts has been a mixed blessing – allowing charities unprecedented growth and a wider client base but bringing new pressures to bear.[23] However, the process was far from clear cut. What appears to be key is the structure that voluntary organisations adopt, and how focused they are on core values and objectives. Increasing professionalisation, for example, can offset some of the bureaucratic constraints and can keep even huge organisations responsive. Some charities adopted a 'federal' approach – sharing support services such as HR while enabling otherwise independent local agencies to respond to local need.

Contract delivery is also far from incompatible with the involvement of volunteers. Rainer, which attracts more than 85% of its funds from statutory contracts, have as many

23 D. W. Scott and L. Russell, "Contracting: the experience of service delivery agencies" in M. Harris and C. Rochester (eds.) *Voluntary organisations and social policy in Britain: perspectives on change and choice* (Basingstoke: Palgrave Macmillan, 2001)

24 NCVO, *United Kingdom Voluntary Sector Almanac 2006* (London: NCVO, 2006)

volunteers as paid staff. They deliver different roles and are able to complement the work that paid staff do. We combine professional criminal justice workers with volunteer mentors – and both have a key role to play. People respond strongly to someone who is spending time with them because they want to – sometimes when everyone else in their life is being paid to be there. And importantly, many of these volunteers are drawn from the local community, engaging them in the local response to offending but also giving them a better understanding of the causes of crime and hopefully builds confidence in the criminal justice system as a whole. Critics of contracting are right to place a high value on volunteers – but that simply means that volunteers should be equally valued within contracts, not that contracting should be written off altogether.

A more subtle argument against contracting is that it subverts charities' objectives and leads them to deliver services as required by commissioners rather than services needed by those they support. This is particularly a risk for charities that come to be heavily dependent on government funds for their survival. Not only has public money now taken over as the major source of funding for the voluntary sector, but most statutory funding is now provided under contract rather than as a grant.[24] A recent example might be the huge expansion of drug treatment services through the criminal justice system. Drug treatment agencies that had qualms about forcing people into treatment or who felt help should be available to all were faced with cutting themselves off from the main funding streams or swallowing their fears in order to grow.

I have no doubt that such situations do occur, and could occur under NOMS but the analysis is flawed. Charities are not docile recipients of government largesse – we play an active role in shaping policy and spending priorities as well as simply carrying out the work. A vibrant voluntary sector must therefore include a campaigning role – the 'watchdog of state' as some term it – as well as a service delivery role. We need to use evidence from our services to inform the policy-making and commissioning processes.

But again, some question whether this is compromised by the increase in funding from government. Will the watchdog really be willing to 'bite the hand that feeds it' and risk losing contracts by speaking out? In response, I would argue that just as the 'charity sector' is made up of multiple organisations with different priorities and approaches so is the statutory sector. Agencies may be dependent on statutory money, but this money may be drawn from numerous different agencies across local and national government, quangos and funding agencies. By spreading the load in this way we become less dependent on individual agencies. At the same time government has clearly set out the right for charities to campaign and voice concerns without the fear of losing funding – backed up by the Compact between statutory and voluntary agencies. This principle has already been tested successfully and, if properly policed, should give organisations the confidence to speak out. Perhaps the most important way to ensure that subversion or 'mission drift' doesn't occur is to make sure that commissioning is evidence-based and takes proper account of the needs of the end user. This is easier said than done, but a first vital step is to ensure that providers are given a role in feeding into commissioning priorities and service development at the planning stage and that commissioning decisions are clearly based on 'what works' rather than process measures.

In short, it is not contracting *per se* that erodes charitable strengths, it is bad contracting. The recent contestability prospectus committed to longer-term contracts over annual ones and also contracts using more standardised terms (which given that up to 40% of charitable staff time can be spent on negotiating or reporting against contracts) is a vital step. These are both welcome developments but what is most important is introducing *smarter* contracts. It is when charities are judged against numbers through the door or by simplistic tick box measures

——— ——— ——— ——— ——— ———

People respond strongly to someone who is spending time with them because they want to – sometimes when everyone else in their life is being paid to be there.

——— ——— ——— ——— ———

25 Susan R. Bernstein, *Managing Contracted Services in the Nonprofit Agency: Administrative, Ethical and Political Issues* (Philadelphia: Temple University Press, 1992)

26 The other founding organisation of what is today Rainer

that the arguments outlined above begin to bite. There should be clear accountability but the measurement of success needs to be high-level, allowing some 'wiggle room' to innovate and to maintain those vital relationships with the people we are working with. A major study of contracting between government and charities in New York found that both sides resorted to 'game playing' to work around poorly designed agreements.[25] Why can't we avoid that from the start, identify the things which are going to have the biggest impact and jointly agree the targets which will make sure we deliver?

For those who are worried about the independence of criminal justice VCOs being eroded as they take on more work for the Home Office, it is again worth turning to the history books. In the mid 1800s, the Philanthropic Society was in internal debate about accepting funding from government.[26] At the time the reform school was proving successful (claiming a startling 5% re-offending rate) and was attracting interest from the Home Secretary, local magistrates and prison governors. The trustees recommended that:

"in the future it be made a regulation… that upon the payment of every hundred pounds… the criminal boy recommended shall be admitted into the Institution provided the case shall appear to the Committee to be within the spirit and regulations of the Establishment."

Faced with the opportunity to expand the numbers of people they worked with by accepting government funds, they took the perfectly reasonable step of accepting referrals which fit the purposes of the charity. I understand the financial pressures that modern organisations face but is it really so different today? Developing new areas of work should not be at the cost of the charity's values or objectives. Staff, volunteers, trustees and clients all have a shared sense of what a particular organisation stands for and the promise of lucrative contracts will not overrule that.

A question of trust
The final concern that has been raised about voluntary organisations' involvement in NOMS is the impact this will have on their relationship with those they support. I have mentioned

the trust that charities are able to inspire a number of times, particularly with those who are or have been excluded from mainstream services and whose main contact with the state is through custody. Some fear that such relationships of trust will be undermined if charities take on a role in offender management – perhaps having to report back on client contact, failure to attend appointments and so on. Others feel that the enforcement role should be kept completely separate from providing support.

As with contracting generally, this is a choice that each charity must take individually. For me, it seems that relationships of trust are based on honesty, consistency and respect. Rainer already provides services such as probation education or Intensive Supervision and Surveillance Programmes which require those taking part to meet stringent rules. Yet there is no lack of trust between our workers and those they support. We can respect the people we work with, without respecting aggressive behaviour or breaches of the rules that have already been agreed. The young people and young adults we work with often value clear rules and consistent values. Services must be designed with the end user in mind and some may only work on a voluntary basis. But to suggest that trust is incompatible with reporting requirements is misguided.

Conclusion

In some ways the current situation reminds me of the debates about Secure Training Centres (STCs) for young offenders some years ago, at which time I was a member of the Youth Justice Board. The initial proposals from Michael Howard were met with anger from voluntary organisations who wanted nothing to do with locking 12-14 year olds up. Despite the change in government and the Youth Justice reforms in 1998 the proposals still remained intact. Two STCs were already under construction by private providers and the YJB approached the VCOs to see if they would be willing to get involved in the three other planned STCs. The answer was a firm no.

Yet with hindsight, it seems that those voluntary agencies' involvement might have lead to a very different approach to STCs than we now have. A charity-run STC might be more focused on the needs of the young person, provide better support and a less punitive environment. Its success might have convinced government to make the approach more widespread and helped avoid the current record levels of young people in custody. Of course, it might have achieved none of these things but my point is, we'll never know – VCOs did not take the opportunity to prove that they had an alternative approach that would work.

As we wait for the detailed proposals on NOMS to be set out, VCOs have to have faith in the work that we do. If we genuinely believe that we can provide successful projects that can help turn individual lives around and benefit whole communities we need to back those convictions with action. We do need to be clear about the risks and the conditions under which such projects will be a success. But that means engaging with the process from the start and setting out a positive vision of how we can have the greatest impact. That is what the private sector is doing, and in a different way what the current probation and prison services are doing. We need to enter the debate with these groups and with government.

Two hundred years ago a similar debate was entered into by some of the leading philanthropists of the time. They felt there must be a better way to work with those caught up in the criminal justice system and that voluntary action could have a greater impact than what was currently in place. Frederick Rainer felt the same in 1876 when faced with the experiences of persistent offenders. We need to have the same conviction today.

Chapter 3: The transformation of public services – the voluntary and community sector and the criminal justice system

By Stuart Etherington

Much has been written about the role of the voluntary and community sector (VCS) and the delivery of public services. This is an important issue and one which deserves the attention that has been focused on it. Elsewhere in this publication contributors discuss the specific contribution that voluntary and community organisations (VCOs) can make in the criminal justice system, and others address some of the practical implications and issues if this agenda is to be taken forward effectively. In this essay I want to concentrate on some of the more philosophical issues that also need to be considered. It can be very easy to focus on how to go down the route of taking on more and bigger contracts, and to identify and address legitimate concerns about how those contracts are managed. But I believe that it is also essential that we are absolutely clear about what we are trying to achieve by taking on the delivery of public services - and in this instance, specifically in helping to achieve improvements to the criminal justice system – and that we understand the implications of our engagement.

Therefore, in this essay, I will address the following three themes:

- the importance of achieving a transformation in the way public services are delivered, not just a transfer
- the ways in which VCOs can contribute to this agenda, particularly through their wider role as campaigners and advocates and through the provision of support and advice, and
- the impact on the VCS, considering the importance of independence and mission, value, capacity, and ethics.

Transformation

The aim of public service reform should not simply be about providing cheaper services – although making better use of taxpayers' money is of course important. The driving aim must be to achieve a genuine, lasting and positive transformation in the public services that people receive. In my view, if we are to achieve that public sector commissioners need to change the way services are designed and managed. Not only do they need to work with external partners – and the VCS is an extremely important external partner – but they need to rethink *how* they work with external partners. Government needs to develop a better understanding of how VCOs can contribute not just to the delivery of public services, but to the reform of those services, and transformation in the experience of service users.

So what do I mean when I talk about transformation and what is it that VCOs in particular can bring to the table? In some quarters there appears to be a belief that simply transferring existing services out of the public sector to another provider will achieve more efficient and effective services - through the market mechanisms of competition and choice. A straightforward transfer of services out of the public sector is an option. And if this is the route that government wants to go down, then some VCOs will undoubtedly want to play a part. Many VCOs believe that even within the constraints of a standard public sector contract they can still provide a better service to users.

However, such a transfer will only provide some marginal benefits to users and communities, unless you assume that the failings are in the public sector *per se*. I do not accept this premise. I do not believe that all public services are inefficient or ineffective: many are very good. Where public services are poor it is not simply because they are in the public sector, it is because the wrong model of delivery is driving them. Therefore the first thing that needs to be done is to change the model of delivery.

Politicians on all sides constantly refer to the need to make services more user-focused. However, little progress on this has been made because there is a tension between two competing political agendas. On the one hand government wants to create services which are tailored to the needs and preferences of the full range of users. On the other hand, the efficiency agenda has been interpreted in a very narrow way, and rewards those who focus on economic savings and throughput, rather than those who achieve more effective services. A more effective service may bring short-term economic gains, but in many cases the gains will be longer term. So, the second thing that needs to be done is for a more sophisticated understanding of efficiency to be applied in the public sector.

The need for these changes is evident: VCOs seek to bring new ideas and additional benefits to the services they provide, but express frustration that the conventional approaches to commissioning and procurement followed by the public sector limit the extent to which services can actually be changed to better meet public need. The current focus on transfer and cost savings has meant that commissioners in the public sector tend to opt for delivery by a few large service providers, excluding smaller, specialist or locally based organisations. The existing model may, at best, provide consistent services for the majority, but it has inbuilt serious weaknesses. It is less likely to address the needs of vulnerable, harder to reach users who need more specialist or different services; it is unlikely to lead to the development of more holistic services, which understand and meet the whole needs of individuals; it offers little scope for investment in researching and developing new solutions; and it does not support innovation nor the piloting of new services.

To achieve a real transformation commissioners need new and more flexible approaches to defining service needs and how solutions to those needs are designed and commissioned. It means going substantially beyond simply offering people a choice of different services, or different providers. It also goes beyond consulting users or communities about the services they would like. It is about working with local communities to identify what the service need is, to enable service users and other experts in the field to contribute to the debate about the best solutions to a particular service need and only then to consider how that service should actually be delivered.

What contribution can the VCS make?

Many across the sector, including NCVO, have argued that VCOs can play a crucial role in both shaping and delivering public services that better meet the needs of individuals and communities. Therefore one very positive aspect of this reform agenda has been the recognition in government of the role that VCOs can play in public service delivery. Much attention is given to the VCS' role in direct provision of services and I do not intend to add to that debate here. But many VCOs would argue that of at least as much importance are their roles in providing:

* advocacy – lobbying and campaigning to ensure that the voice of particular communities is heard, particularly to inform the way that needs are identified and then how services are designed and delivered
* advice and information – to help individuals and communities understand and access the services available to them.

These multiple roles should be one of the strengths of the VCS in public service delivery. For most VCOs that deliver services, campaigning and advocacy are an important part of what they do. Their campaigning and advocacy work is strengthened and has legitimacy because they also have direct service delivery experience. And the way they deliver services is informed and strengthened by their direct role in advice and advocacy. In short the roles are complementary. In addition, there are many VCOs that have no interest in delivering public services but who still want to contribute to a debate on a particular service. Through their advice and advocacy work they have an under-standing of the concerns and needs of particular communities, and these VCOs may have a crucial role in representing the needs and interests of communities who might otherwise not be heard.

But government funders can fail to appreciate the benefits that these multiple roles bring. The broader contribution can be overlooked, or even viewed as inappropriate. Some argue that there is a conflict of interest if a VCO wants to both advocate for a certain approach, or be consulted on or contribute to decisions about how a service should be designed and delivered, and then want to bid for the contract to deliver that service. This separation (in the minds of some parts of government) of service delivery from campaigning and advocacy is problematic because it does not reflect the way VCOs operate. It is important that commissioners understand that the VCS roles of advocacy, support and advice giving contribute directly to public service delivery. Any potential conflict of interest can then be acknowledged and managed through the commissioning and procurement processes.

The impact on the sector

Independence and mission
The current political environment offers greater opportunities to the VCS and we need to make sure that we take advantage of these opportunities. But, I do not believe that VCOs should have a role in all circumstances and at any cost. Important as the public service reform agenda is, it is only one aspect of the sector's contribution to society. We need to ensure a balance between this and our wider role in supporting and promoting civil society.

VCOs are independent organisations. This needs to be reflected throughout our engagement in public services. Public service delivery should contribute to the delivery of a VCO's own mission and help it to better meet the needs of their users and members. And where VCOs take on public service delivery, it must be done in ways that respect the independence of the organisation and the expertise and knowledge that they contribute, and the services they provide must be properly costed and paid for. In short, VCOs should take on public service delivery on their own terms and in order to help meet their own objectives: public service delivery is a means to an end for VCOs, it is not the end in itself.

Of course, there is always the risk that an over-expansion into public service delivery can skew the focus of an organisation and the original mission can become marginal. NCVO

27 Ann Blackmore, *Standing apart, working together: A study of the myths and realities of voluntary and community sector independence* (London: NCVO, 2004).

considered these risks in 2004.[27] Our report made it clear that engaging with government does not automatically undermine the sector's independence; it is a question of how the relationship (and the contract) is managed, and the extent to which VCOs give careful thought to the possible implications before they enter into partnerships or contracts.

Distinctive value

If we are seeking to bring VCS experience and perspectives into public service delivery in order to help facilitate transformation, then we need to ensure that the value the VCS brings is not lost. It is often because they operate in different ways to the public sector that VCOs can add value to public services. Traditionally the voluntary sector focus is on working from the bottom up: good voluntary sector services are those which emerge to meet a need, to fill a gap, and which are informed by the needs and preferences of those using the service. As such they need to be flexible and responsive, in a way that a single provider, from whatever sector, would find difficult.

There is a danger that the nature of the contract itself can undermine what a VCO wants to bring to a service, for example, if it is overly prescriptive about processes rather than outcomes. It is therefore important that our statutory partners understand and value the differences between the ways VCOs and the public sector operate.

But there are also issues that a VCO needs to take into account itself. Whilst an organisation may be very good at providing services on a small scale to a particular community or niche market, it may not be able to replicate the same service on a larger scale. It may lack the capacity and skills to do so. And where a VCO does have the skills and capacity to take on large scale service delivery, scaling the service up may cause it to lose what made it effective in the first place: VCOs need to consider the risk that they may become, or be perceived, as monolithic and inflexible as the statutory sector.

Funding and capacity

The public service delivery agenda has made available increased sources of funding to many VCOs. However we should be wary of seeing this as an opportunity in itself: it is only an opportunity in so far as it enables VCOs to help deliver better outcomes for the individuals and communities they exist to support. Government funding is, quite legitimately, focused on government priorities. But those will not be the same as the priorities of all VCOs. We need to give careful thought to how VCOs that contribute more widely to civil society are supported. Or indeed those that have different ideas to government about what services should be provided, or how they should be provided.

We also need to consider the long-term impact on sustainability of increased funding: significant expansion and hence dependence on public service contracts can make an organisation vulnerable to changes in government policy priorities and funding priorities.

VCOs also need to be clearer about their objectives in service delivery: is the purpose to deliver a service and generate income, or is it to ensure a better service is widely available? For example, a wider engagement with VCOs in the designing and commissioning of services may mean that the solutions designed and piloted by VCOs become funded as part of the mainstream and will not remain within the VCS. Whilst there are issues about how such investment in service development is funded, it is equally true that if it results in a better service for a larger number of people, then it is still a successful outcome for both the VCO and those with whom it works.

Ethical issues and public trust and confidence
The final point I wish to raise is about ethics. Does it matter if VCOs – who are after all civil society organisations – take on roles that could change the nature of their relationship with those that have until now been considered their beneficiaries or clients? For example, VCOs may take contracts that require them to make recommendations about a person's eligibility for certain state benefits, when in the past the role of the VCO was to advise or support people who were trying to access benefits. Clearly there is potential for this to be a major issue in relation to criminal justice. Some national charities see their role as providing advice, support services and information to offenders, but would never want to move into a role even close to making decisions that might affect the liberty of an individual. Other charities have indicated that they would have no problem with

such a role.

The question is, should this be a matter for individual charities, or is this an issue on which the actions of some charities could have a serious impact on the way that the public perceive the sector more widely? We need to be realistic that in certain areas a greater role in public service delivery could pose a serious challenge to public trust and confidence in the sector.

Conclusion

The government's agenda to reform public services offers huge opportunities to VCOs to ensure better services and better outcomes for those they work with and for. But if this is to happen, government needs to recognise and reward the wider contribution VCOs can make to public service reform.

The reforms needed for procurement processes have already been identified in the Treasury's 2002 Cross Cutting Review, and reiterated by the NAO and PAC reports, but there remains the need for a stronger commitment to implementation. This includes funding the full cost of providing a properly defined service, ensuring that risk is fairly shared, providing longer term funding where appropriate and ensuring that monitoring requirements are proportionate. It is to be hoped that the Action Plan that government is due to publish in autumn 2006 will help truly embed these reforms at both the national and local level. But if VCOs are not involved in service definition and design, as well as service delivery, then the scope for transformation will be extremely limited.

We should also enter this arena with a degree of caution. It would be naive to assume that services will always be designed and contracts offered in the ways that we think they should be. And we need to understand the risks that may be associated with taking on a greater role in public service delivery. We need to improve our skills in negotiating, and sometimes in saying no. Because as I have already said, public service delivery is a means to an end; it is not the end in itself. And just because we are invited to take on a service, it does not mean we should. VCOs form an independent sector that plays a number of different roles in civil society. Public service delivery is an important role, but it is only one of the roles performed by the VCS.

Chapter 4: From ashtrays to enterprises? Third sector involvement in the criminal justice system

By Nick Aldridge and Stephen Bubb

Commentators ranging from ancient philosophers to the present Home Secretary agree that rehabilitation, not just retribution, is crucial to the success of a criminal justice system. Third sector organisations lead pioneering work in providing young offenders with an alternative to crime. NOMS' commissioning strategy must enable this work, and the ethos that guides it, to move from the margins to the mainstream.

What is the point of the criminal justice system? Thinkers have suggested various answers. Plato, for instance, viewed justice as a form of personal rationality and spiritual good health, to be nurtured through the educational interventions of an enlightened state. Perhaps, therefore, the primary role of the criminal justice system is rehabilitative: to educate offenders into more "rational" behaviour.

More recently, Hart characterised the foundations of the legal system as adherence, particularly by public officials, to some ultimate standards against which particular laws can be assessed.[28] Any legal system must pursue and protect these lofty standards if it is to survive. Others have variously argued that the primary role of the criminal justice system should be retributive, preventative, or restorative.

In his July Action Plan to reform the Home Office, John

28 Herbert L. Hart, *The Concept of Law,* (Oxford: Oxford University Press, 1961).

29 Home Office,
*From Improvement to
Transformation*, (London:
Home Office, 2006), p. 3.

Reid emphatically defined the core purpose of his department as "protecting the public".[29] This fits within a wider political strategy of "rebalancing the criminal justice system in favour of the law-abiding majority and the victim", a move that has caused nervousness among many members of the judicial system, and in third sector sector oganisations that fear a retreat from the rehabilitative agenda.

Will a rebalancing of the system involve a further shift towards retribution rather than rehabilitation, particularly when government might be seen as reacting to tabloid demands? Longer sentences and more prison places are unlikely to have a lasting positive effect on levels of crime, particularly if this leads to further overcrowding, strains on the probation service, and a reduction in the levels of support available for tackling prisoners' problems such as illiteracy, addictions, and poor mental health.

In July John Reid announced that 8,000 more prison places in England and Wales would be provided, taking the total up to almost 90,000 by 2012. The latest projections from the Home Office suggest that even this total number of places could fall short of requirements.

The view of some acevo members on this construction parallels that of many environmentalists on road building: 'solving crime-related problems with prisons is like solving smoking-related problems with ashtrays.' Long-term success will depend on tackling the problem further upstream.

Juliet Lyon, the director of the Prison Reform Trust, called instead on the government to, "Tackle the drug addiction, alcohol-fuelled disorder and neglect of mental illness that are causing this hyperinflation of men, women and children in our prisons."

Government has rarely articulated with any strength the

Third sector organisations lead pioneering work in providing young offenders with an alternative to crime.

need for rehabilitation and support as an integral part of the crime-cutting agenda. An obvious case can – and should - be made that the majority of crime is committed by ex-offenders, and repeat patterns of offending can only be broken through interventions that address the issues driving offenders to crime.

To be fair to the government, this problem is well-recognised, if not yet well-addressed. Martin Narey, now CEO of Barnardo's, previously ran the National Offender Management Service (NOMS). Heavily critical of the "violent and evil" culture of some prisons, Narey also drew attention last year to the complex challenges involved in providing rehabilitation for prisoners:

"90% of those entering prison [in 2000] were recognised as displaying one or more forms of mental disorder – that is, alcohol addiction, drug addiction, psychosis, neurosis or personality disorder." [30]

Put another way, male and female prisoners are respectively 14 and 35 times more likely to suffer multiple mental health disorders than the general population. Within this context, rehabilitative interventions will need to be sophisticated and carefully managed.

The Home Office's action plan, regardless of its tough tone, also acknowledges this need. It remarks of NOMS:

"We will focus its headquarters on the job of commissioning high-quality services for managing offenders, and driving up the performance of the probation and prison services. This will involve…opening more services up to competition from the voluntary and private sectors." [31]

Other Labour thinkers have gone further. In a speech last year to Centrepoint, a young people's agency, Stephen Byers MP called for a national "Strong Foundations" programme owned by young people, rather than Whitehall, to steer young people away from underachievement and from crime.[32] Such an initiative would need to be supported actively by the relevant third sector organisations.

The Conservative party, under David Cameron's leadership, is also placing renewed emphasis on the need for a "second chance culture" for ex-offenders and drug addicts, in which the

30 Martin Narey quoted in Vikram Dodd, "Cell conditions 'gross' for 20%", *The Guardian*, 8 February 2005.

31 Home Office (2006), p.9.

32 Stephen Byers MP, Centrepoint Anniversary Lecture, 8 February 2005 http://www.socialexclusionunit.gov.uk/events.asp?id=559&pld=19.

33 David Cameron speech, 18 January 2006 http://politics.guardian. co.uk/conservatives/ story/0,9061,1689389,00. html.

skills of the third sector will play a leading part.[33]

More immediately, a long-awaited NOMS "prospectus" of opportunities for independent providers may place increased emphasis on the role of third sector organisations within the criminal justice system. It is widely acknowledged that a number of advantages enjoyed by third sector organisations make them well-placed to steer offenders away from crime. Among the most compelling of these advantages are the following:

1. User-focus: they are mission-driven, and have relatively little incentive to compromise on service quality in order to meet other requirements
2. Flexibility: they can work across government silos to connect otherwise disparate policy priorities and funding streams, for example bridging the gap between correctional and employment-related services
3. Social capital: by engaging volunteers and the wider community in their work, they can promote better understanding of ex-offenders and speed their reintegration into local communities.

In practice, as well as in theory, third sector organisations provide some of the most positive interventions aimed at the rehabilitation of offenders, particularly young people.

Rathbone's "Prove It" Programme

In Manchester, Rathbone has developed a demand-led engagement strategy for young offenders and disengaged young people. The agency works in partnership with Youth Offending Teams, (YOT), Intensive Supervision & Surveillance Programmes, (ISSP) and Connexions, from whom referrals are generated.

Through an Outreach Programme, Rathbone is pro-active in finding young people that for many reasons do not wish to become engaged, this accounts for 25% of their learners.

The programme, named 'Prove It', is specifically designed for young people to achieve nationally recognised qualifications in Key Skills, Literacy, Language and Numeracy, to assist with the transition into accessing more formal education and/or employment.

They have had 100% success in achieving two or more qualifications and 70% of learners successfully complete their ISSP/YOT supervision orders.

The success of the programme can be attributed to the learner to staff ratio, two staff to a maximum of six learners, engaged on the Prove It programme and the one to one provision for those young people who are not quite ready for full engagement. The Prove It, e2e and Outreach provision, are dovetailed within the centre ensuring all the needs of the learners can be addressed, thus adding value to all the programmes.

The challenge for third sector organisations, as in so many areas of public service reform, lies in helping the government to move this kind of intervention from the margins of correctional services into mainstream provision. This involves many challenges, such as the relative lack of integration between welfare to work schemes and the probation service, which has led to the criminal justice system becoming unnecessarily isolated from positive job-placement activities.

Although charities already provide services to prisoners, many children's charities have expressed serious reservations about getting more closely involved in the management of a system they regard as failing young people. Others, however, are bolder. Rebecca Pritchard, Director of Services at Centrepoint, said last year that "charities have a lot to offer", and although "Locking up kids does not do them any good… charities should risk taking on new things." Some organisations are already putting this into practice.

CfBT Education Trust: learning for prisoners

In partnership with G4S, the CfBT Education Trust runs the Learning Centre for up to 80 young people aged 12-17 at Oakhill Secure Training Centre. A newly built project, the Centre opened in August 2004 and to date around 500 boys and girls have received a high quality education from CfBT's staff team. CfBT, along with the local Health Care Trust are part of the G4S Senior Management team in Oakhill.

In their last visit to the centre, Ofsted commended CfBT's work, particularly the leadership provided, the high quality of teaching

34 www.madeinjail.com

and learning and the impressive range of qualifications achieved by trainees – over 4000 accredited units in the last 12 months. They also recognised the contribution made by CfBT's specialist team of Education Link Workers who work closely with Youth Offending Teams and G4S staff, to place 80% of the young people leaving Oakhill into schools, colleges and jobs in their home areas.

The third sector's emphasis on skills, training and employment can give prisoners and ex-offenders an alternative to crime. Drawing on examples from abroad, the concept of social enterprise may provide a way of giving them the confidence to take it up. The Cooperativa Sociale Seriarte Ecologica, founded in Rome in 1988, aims to help prisoners reintegrate into the economy through a social firm that sells T-shirts. Its eyecatching website provides an illustration of how prisoners' experiences can be turned into an asset.[34]

Silvio Palermo, a founding member of the cooperative, reports:

"I went to jail in '81 on a conviction for terrorism. Having renounced political violence I was released in '87 with two other inmates. We had started making t-shirts in jail as a bit of fun. But when we were out the former director of the Rebibbia Jail in Rome invited the three of us to help him set up a social cooperative. We began to make t-shirts with inmates in the Casal del Marmo young offenders institution. The main problem for us had been finding a job and a new place in society. This cooperative gave us the opportunity. We have now worked for 18 years with over 50 members of the cooperative. All are former prisoners. Thanks to recent television coverage, we have had the opportunity to promote our activity and increase sales. What we need in Italy is more third sector projects like this one!"

Closer to home, social enterprises ranging from Hill Holt Wood on the edge of Lincolnshire through to the Trailblazers mentoring programme in Feltham Young Offenders Institution, alongside well-established and highly effective charities such as Rainer, are helping to steer young people away from crime and into employment.

Despite their impressive results, many such organisations are struggling to survive within the current commissioning environment. In a report last year for the Barrow Cadbury Trust, Greg Parston criticised the criminal justice system's overall approach as "frustrating, unhelpful and even damaging" for young people.[35] The report called for better mental health services and opportunities to access education and employment for young people.

The experience of C-FAR, led by Trevor Philpott, provides a striking example of how the very best of these services may find it difficult to interact with NOMS.

35 Barrow Cadbury Commission, *Lost in Transition: A Report of the Barrow Cadbury Commission on Young Adults and the Criminal Justice System* (London: Barrow Cadbury Trust, 2005).

36 Martin Brookes and John Copps, *Surer Funding: Acevo Commission of Inquiry Report* (London: Acevo, 2004).

Formally based at Highampton in North Devon, C-FAR worked to help young adult offenders break out from the cycle of crime and exclusion. Many of the young people who undertook the programme suggested that it had saved their lives.

The outcomes achieved were repeatedly affirmed by professionals (Prison, Probation and Police officers, Judges and Magistrates), trainees and their families. Re-offending rates were more than 30% lower than the national average and for those that did re-offend levels and type of offending were also lower.

Just over 40% of referrals were made by the Courts as an alternative to custody with Judges publicly applauding the programme. Based upon figures from the 2002 Social Exclusion Unit, C-FAR estimated it had saved the Treasury over £12million.

Sadly, following repeated delays in the introduction of NOMS budgets, the trustees took the decision to go into voluntary liquidation. The alternative was to seek more charitable funding, but in light of the number of referrals, this was seen by Trustees as morally indefensible.

Now working as unpaid volunteers, Trevor and three former managers are waiting to resurrect the programme as a new company, Life Change UK. According to its management, "the critical factor remains the willingness or otherwise of the criminal justice system to make an appropriate contribution towards the costs of future delivery."

Surer Funding, an extensive research study published by acevo in 2004, showed how the insecurity, unpredictability, and basic unfairness of many forms of statutory funding are causing a crisis in third sector capacity.[36] Short-term funding streams, subject to continual review, have made it very difficult for third sector organisations to invest in the development of services and staff, or expand to take on a greater role in service delivery and reform. The report showed that, as a result of these short-comings, citizens receive services that are not as reliable or high quality, as they could and should be, and government bodies achieve poor value for taxpayers' money in commissioning those services.

Fragmentation has also proved a problem. Many acevo members working with prisons have expressed frustration at the apparent lack of coordination in their procurement processes. They point to prisons that work with many different voluntary sector providers, each delivering a similar service, without pro-viding stable funding for any one of them. Liverpool Prison, for example, currently works with 91 separate voluntary organisa-tions. In common with many other areas of third sector provi-sion, providers have difficulty negotiating contracts that provide a stable and fully funded basis for service delivery and develop-ment. Besides leading to inefficiencies in delivery, the system has prevented third sector work reaching the mainstream of the criminal justice system. In recognition of this problem, the Prison Service has shown increasing willingness to improve its procurement and contracting processes.

The introduction of more coherent and coordinated com-missioning by NOMS, when it materialises, should provide an opportunity to address these shortcomings. The introduction of more contestability may give third sector organisations the chance to compete for a more central role in the criminal justice system, to the benefit of ex-offenders and the wider society into which, at present, many fail to integrate.

NOMS must overcome its teething problems and build the foundations of a system in which truly effective interven-tions for ex-offenders can thrive. Three principles should guide this system.

First, third sector organisations – both service provid-ers and advocacy organisations – must be involved upstream in commissioning decisions. Their experience, gained both through delivery and through consultation, should form the basis of a more holistic approach to offender management.

Second, third sector organisations must have a genuine chance to compete for service delivery contracts, including mainstream contracts aimed at the rehabilitation of prisoners. There should be no inbuilt presumption that the status quo provides the ideal model, and no tilting of the playing field towards existing providers. Commissioning and procurement timetables must enable and encourage innovative cross-sector partnerships to emerge. Capacity building interventions should be encouraged for those organisations on the verge of entering the mainstream market.

Third, the procurement models used must steer Regional Offender Managers away from the short-termism, insecurity and fragmentation that has characterised financial relationships in the past. Drawing on recent reforms in Job Centre Plus, which has moved to 3 and 5 year contracts, NOMS should make sure its arrangements are stable enough for providers from all sectors to provide efficient services, and have the flexibility to allow innovation and improvement. As Joyce Moseley, Rainer's chief executive, succinctly puts it, contracts must be longer, fairer, and smarter.

Chapter 5: Just another service provider? The voluntary sector's place in the National Offender Management Service

By Julian Corner

At the inception of the National Offender Management Service, voluntary organisations were told publicly that they had a great deal more to offer, and behind closed doors they were encouraged to 'think big'. The truisms of voluntary sector "innovation" and "expertise" were dusted down, but new ideas were also introduced. Larger organisations started to eye probation's core business and think previously unthinkable thoughts about providing offender supervision and even running prisons. Small to medium-sized organisations saw accelerated opportunities to become regional or national providers themselves. Offender services were described as a 'growth market' for the voluntary sector. Some of these aspirations were further encouraged by collaborative discussions with private providers, whose own models of growth allowed some voluntary organisations to see a way of breaking through previously impermeable glass ceilings.

The costs of such growth are always a vexed topic for voluntary organisations. There is a fine line between increased impact and compromised values and this is nowhere more evident that in the voluntary sector's work with offenders. As voluntary organisations take on ever larger chunks of the system to run, it becomes critical to reflect on the implications for these organisations of becoming instruments of the state. Should voluntary organisations really be viewed as equivalent providers to the public and private sector? Is this really the best use of the voluntary sector's contribution? What are the ethical and moral dimensions for organisations that are led by values and founded on relationships with service users?

The purpose of this essay is to argue that NOMS will need to foster a plurality of relationships with offenders if it is to succeed in reducing re-offending. The model of a single offender manager overseeing a single plan within a single system is seductive in its promised focus on the needs of the offender, but it is based on the colossal assumption that the offender will be willing and able to engage. It does not acknowledge the extent to which the offender population is borne out of vulnerable people's alienation from compulsory, coercive and punishing statutory systems. The voluntary sector has a key role to play here in offering trusted relationships and interventions that are not fully implicated in the system. But this is not the direction that NOMS is currently signalling. So far, it appears to be diversifying its provider base in order to strengthen its grip on providers, in order to provide a more streamlined, commissioner-led service. There is a very real risk that it will do so at the cost of many voluntary organisations' relationship with the very people whom NOMS needs to reach. If voluntary organisations are to make in-roads into probation services, they should be given opportunities to offer radically different approaches, rather than adopting the methods of the state. NOMS will only reach maturity as an organisation when it can tolerate, hold and support such differences of method and relationship within one commissioning framework.

From the beginnings of its work in the criminal justice system, the voluntary sector has played both a tangible and symbolic role. It has reached out to the most vulnerable people, not just because the state was failing to do so, but in order to demonstrate that wider society would not turn its back, even when fellow citizens had contravened its rules. The voluntary sector's embodiment of a concerned society outside of the criminal justice system was an ideological and humanitarian stand for individuals who had been rendered full-blown objects of the state. Whether this voluntary involvement acted as a witness to decency, or worked more proactively to secure that decency, the result was a relationship between the voluntary organisation and the individual that was utterly distinct from that between state and individual. It was a relationship that still exists today between many voluntary organisations and their 'clients', based fundamentally on a belief in the individual's humanity and a conviction that no one is ever beyond the pale. Although these values can be implicit in the state's relationship with the individual, the state's primary duty is to make the individual subject to statutory requirement.

The tension between the roles of advocate and enforcer characterised the evolution of the probation service throughout the twentieth century. Probation inherited its former duty to 'advise, assist and befriend' out of the nationalisation of voluntary advocacy work with offenders. Nationalisation led to the state delivering value-led, humanitarian work with offenders that was perhaps only possible because probation services were overseen in local areas by local boards. When the Government created a National Probation Service in the late nineties, the tension inherent in the state as 'befriender' and the state as 'punisher' was felt to be intolerable. This was most obviously because central government was unable to reconcile its desire to deliver strong simple messages to the victims of crime with the more complex task of tackling crime through its causes. Even though it had always been probation's role, 'befriending' was caricatured as symptomatic of a service gone soft and it became an almost inevitable casualty of the creation of the national service.

It is significant that the voluntary sector did not die out when befriending was nationalised. Much of its focus shifted to prisons and to concerns about prisoners who were women or who were very young. The voluntary sector developed and promoted a crucial perspective on why people ended up in prison, as well as asking what to do once they were there. The former was a perspective unattainable by the state, with its departmental buck-passing and silo delivery. As such, the voluntary sector was able to highlight the use of prison as a dustbin for the homeless, the drug addicted, the mentally ill, battered women, alienated young black men, and above all, people with so many problems that their lives had descended into chaos. Hundreds of small voluntary organisations were set up to address all of these issues and many more. Through its growing diversity, the voluntary sector came to embody the complex social circumstances that generated our prison and offender population, circumstances otherwise masked by public sector monoliths.

By the time the Social Exclusion Unit (SEU) report *Reducing Re-offending by Ex-prisoners* set the framework for offender rehabilitation in 2002, it was the voluntary sector not the state that was able to define the profile and needs of the offender population.[37] The National Probation Service, on the other hand, had become so fixated on what it called offenders' cognitive deficits that the then Chief Inspector of Probation described it as a 'fetish'. Thousands of people were pushed through uniformly delivered 'cognitive behavioural programmes' in a system that was otherwise apparently oblivious to the wider emotional and logistical impossibility of these people's lives. Only the voluntary sector did not collude in this and only because of its stand was the SEU report possible.

While the state thought that people could be reprogrammed, much of the voluntary sector retained its focus on welfare, sometimes in the face of national probation service cynicism about unevidenced 'do-gooding'. The subsequent evidence that probation's delivery of cognitive behavioural programmes had made little or no impact appears to vindicate pragmatic welfare over more politically palatable strategies of correcting flawed personalities. Most observers now agree that effective practice lies somewhere in the combination of the two. But what this stand-off demonstrates is that the state will almost invariably incline towards solutions that can be delivered on mass through target-driven performance systems *and* that it is fully capable of doing so in the face of common sense. The state is always in danger of collapsing 'what is needed' with 'what can be delivered'. Crucially, the voluntary sector is less at risk of this because it does not have the same responsibility for large numbers of people.

The state will always find it difficult to accept that working with this most disadvantaged and complex of groups is fundamentally messy. It will always want to tidy people's chaos and disarray into pathways, blocks of provision and action plans. In fact, there is nothing wrong with this. The state should aim for

37 Social Exclusion Unit, *Reducing Re-offending by Ex-prisoners* (West Yorkshire: Social Exclusion Unit, 2002).

tidier and more efficient coordination to avoid compounding an individual's chaos with systemic chaos. But this is not the whole story, just as cognitive behavioural programmes were never the whole solution. Unless there is seriously intelligent commissioning behind it, efficient delivery can often be the enemy of effective delivery.

What the SEU report showed most powerfully was that re-offending, and indeed the prison population itself, is a social exclusion issue. As demonstrated in all SEU reports, social exclusion exists at the interface of a system's inability or unwillingness to address the needs of an individual *and* that individual's inability and unwillingness to address their own needs by cooperating with the system. Tidying up the system is half the battle but the Holy Grail is tidying up the person. The assumption of cognitive behavioural programmes was that the system could do the former *and* the latter. Unfortunately, issues of social exclusion rarely lend themselves to efficient delivery mechanisms, and indeed the SEU has found time and again that one-size-fits-all narrow-gauge strategies are part and parcel of what leads to people being excluded and getting into trouble in the first place.

The profile of the prison population alone belies the illusion of an efficient solution. 49 per cent of prisoners have been excluded from school; 50 per cent ran away from home; 20 per cent have been admitted to a mental health hospital; 27 per cent have been in care; and 40 per cent have experienced violence or sexual abuse from a young age. The levels of alienation, distrust and anti-authoritarian anger that such experiences engender might seem sufficient explanation alone for the mental illness, substance misuse and the offending of many. It is perhaps laudable for the state to take responsibility for resolving these problems, but it is also the height of presumption to think that it can legislate for people's trust and acceptance when their only experience of the state and authority has been painful and destructive. This is the very point at which the state needs to acknowledge its limitations and turn to the voluntary sector. But this would require that the state was able to see and reflect on the limitations of its own power and perspective; a rare commodity indeed in a state, especially at times of turbulence and change. It would also require the voluntary sector to be working at its best, with its values fully deployed.

People working in smaller voluntary organisations know to their cost that voluntary engagement with a damaged person can be stressful and uncertain. They can face rejection and anger at any point, and they have to work overtime to maintain appropriate boundaries between themselves and their clients. As a result, many voluntary organisations become almost uniquely expert in living and dealing effectively with the real-life chaos of some people's lives. This is a strain and a complication most statutory organisations and workers would not accept; hence social exclusion. And again, there is nothing particularly wrong with this. Many voluntary organisations build relationships that statutory workers would find impossible to achieve, largely by virtue of the fact that they are not instruments of the state. This is the highly pragmatic pay-off of the unique relationship between many voluntary organisations and individuals described earlier. The values of the voluntary sector translate into very real benefit for both the individual and the state, well beyond that which the state can achieve, both practically *and* politically, on its own.

NOMS talks a great deal about the importance of relationships with offenders, but it still believes that the key relationship can always be delivered through its own Offender Managers. The concept of 'offender management' itself betrays the state's continuing fantasy that the individual can somehow be brought under its control with scientifically targeted evidence-based tools. The re-offending rate suggests otherwise. The revealing choice of the term 'offender management' at the launch of NOMS revealed the instincts of a system that believes it can press buttons in Whitehall that directly and measurably change the behaviours of troubled people on the ground. Of course, the state will always be able to find evidence of success. These are policies and initiatives that are designed to produce impressive numbers. But we rarely hear about the large swathes of people who weren't helped by the policy; the people who were the opportunity cost of the policy; the people who were probably a bit too difficult for the policy. The state suppresses the evidence of its exclusionary practice, because it needs to demonstrate that it has spent our money wisely. Inevitably, voluntary organisations who are prepared to adopt the methods of the state also get caught up in suppressing this evidence because they want to demonstrate their own effectiveness. What emerges in some areas is a 'fourth sector' of organisations who attempt to hold the larger voluntary organisations to account for how they run state contracts and who attempt to catch the human fall-out from those contracts.

There is no denying that many organisations, whose existence depends on the state, are facing a high-wire act to maintain both their integrity and their impact. But it is inaccurate to suggest (using a different analogy) that this is a grey area. Voluntary organisations will certainly be required to assume their place in the relevant referral pathway; they will see each client on the basis of an official assessment of need and at the time allotted in the offender management plan; and they will provide such information as the Offender Manager requires to make difficult decisions about enforcement. That is, of course, unless they are the Offender Manager themselves. In any event, the individual will know that the voluntary organisation wishes to engage with them because the state wishes or requires it. For some offenders, this will not be a problem, so long as they get the help and service they need. But for many excluded people, this is not a relationship they want from their voluntary sector, and there is a considerable risk that they will reject it. Just as the centralisation of the probation service led to the sacrifice of befriending, we now run the real risk that central and regional commissioning of probation's core functions will take the same toll on voluntary sector relationships with offenders.

It is clear that the system needs tidying up. The voluntary sector has been lobbying for this for years. But when, as happened at the first NOMS conference, public, private and voluntary organisations are told "we are all NOMS now", it becomes evident that the messiness of the old system allowed for some diversity of perspective, approach and relationship that NOMS is now capable of sacrificing almost entirely, just as probation signed up almost entirely to cognitive behavioural programmes. It has become the new regime that drives the people at the centre. It has become 'the thing we all do now'.

NOMS commissioners need to reflect very carefully whether their desire to transform the voluntary sector into a useful third provider is indeed the best use of that sector. There is the distinct possibility, as commissioners substitute public with voluntary sector provision, that they will get more of the same. It might look a bit different, have a few bells and tassels not seen in the public sector, but fundamentally it will be the same old specifications delivering the same old relationships. And the voluntary sector working within NOMS is very vulnerable indeed to being shaped and determined in this way. Unlike voluntary organisations working in other sectors, such as Banardos, the British Heart Foundation and the Red Cross, these are not organisations that can use publicly donated funds to 'make their own weather', even as they accept big contracts. They cannot rattle cans for offenders or appeal to grateful beneficiaries. Many are more than 90 per cent dependent on statutory funding. There is nothing wrong in principle with such dependent relationships, but in practice such organisations risk becoming instruments of the state, and thereby risk losing connection with and the trust of their local communities and service users. Just as seriously, commissioners risk hearing their own thinking reflected back to them by compliant organisations that once provided diverse and challenging perspectives. These are risks that need to be managed by commissioners who are alive to the unique value and values of the voluntary sector.

With re-offending shown conclusively to be a social exclusion phenomenon, here is a sector that can reach groups and people like no other. Adopting the tools of flexibility, outreach, trust, confidentiality and agenda-free engagement, voluntary organisations can connect with people who would get nowhere near an accredited programme. Most voluntary organisations also work instinctively across public sector silos, because this is what their clients have to do. As regional rehabilitation 'pathways' are developed, some voluntary organisations are struggling to choose which one to join. They are rushing from pathway to pathway, afraid of falling behind. Others organisations are worried that they work with offenders before the sentence begins and often long after it finishes, and that their wider work will not be recognised because it doesn't fit the commissioning system. Others are worried that the unique social capital that they bring to their work, such as the trust of their service users and local communities, will actually weaken their bids for funding in the face of more commercially attractive proposals.

But these should not be the sector's weaknesses. They are signs of its strength. Many voluntary organisations are already more nuanced and cutting edge than the pathways and the sentencing framework. While some may not look terribly sophisticated, robust or evidence-based, their responsiveness to the individual actually makes NOMS look distinctly old hat in its talk of relationships, holistic delivery and seamless sentences.

The architects of NOMS made a huge leap of faith when they concluded that market-based performance improvement and offender management could together deliver the difference that was needed. Their solution has very obvious merits, but ultimately it seems too process-orientated, too systemic to be convincing at the human level where the fight against reducing re-offending will be played out. It is not too late for a shift in emphasis. NOMS still presents an unprecedented opportunity to empower a currently fragile voluntary sector to take its work to another level and to bring its social inclusion practice fully to bear on an excluded group. This would require NOMS to be open to commissioning approaches and relationships that go against the grain of its instincts to compel and control. It would require NOMS to co-commission creatively across and beyond silos with the NHS, Jobcentre Plus and local authorities. It would require NOMS to commission outcomes rather than service specifications. It would require the offender management model to be fully capable of accommodating divergent relationships with the offender, including key relationships that are confidential from the offender manager. Crucially, it would require commissioners to demonstrate how they had taken the views of service user recipients on board when commissioning services.

The voluntary sector could yet prove to be NOMS' most potent weapon in its battle against re-offending. However the current proposals to upscale its role risk disarming its contribution from the outset. There is nothing to stop voluntary organisations selling their expertise to commissioners on commissioners' terms. For some, this will be the best route. But unless many voluntary organisations are also given full credit for trying to do something quite different, something of which no other sector is now capable, NOMS risks gaining a mixed market but losing the battle to reduce re-offending.

Chapter 6: Working with volunteers and the voluntary sector – some lessons for probation from youth justice

By Rod Morgan

Despite the confusion over the future of the probation service over the past three years, the Carter Report and the various Home Office statements accompanying the emergence of the National Offender Management Service (NOMS)[38] points to the reversal of a trend which concerned me greatly when I was Chief Inspector of Probation.[39] Namely, that the probation service, which grew out of voluntary effort had largely spurned working with volunteers and was allowing partnerships with the voluntary sector – an important distinction, frequently not made and worth emphasising – 'to whither on the vine.'[40] All the evidence available to me during the period 2001-4 indicated that the National Probation Service's (NPS) use of volunteers was in most areas in almost terminal decline and many partnerships with the voluntary sector were under threat, allegedly for want of resources. I thought that trend both odd and counter-productive. It was odd because it was contrary to the then Home Office's target to increase voluntary and community sector activity, including increasing community participation, by 5 per cent by 2006. It was counter-productive because my life-long experience of working with volunteers and the voluntary sector persuaded me that the rationale for involving the voluntary sector in the delivery of services, as set out in

38 In particular this applies to the Discussion Paper, *Developing a NOMS Communities and Civil Renewal Strategy* (London: Home Office, 2005).

39 Patrick Carter (2003); Home Office – *Developing a NOMS Communities and Civil Renewal Strategy* (London: Home Office, 2003).

40 Peter Raynor and Maurice Vanstone, *Understanding community penalties: Probation, policy and social change* (Buckingham: Open University Press, 2002), Chapter 2.

41 HM Treasury, *Cross Cutting Review of the Role of the Voluntary Sector in Public Services Delivery* (London: HM Treasury, 2002).

the *Treasury Cross-Cutting Review* on the topic, is correct.[41] It is worth reminding ourselves how the *Treasury Review* summarised the case for voluntary sector involvement in the delivery of public services:

- The voluntary sector is arguably better capable than either the state or private sectors at delivering certain services to those who are peculiarly marginal, excluded, hard-to-reach and vulnerable – i.e. those citizens who lack market power, who cannot easily articulate their position, who are socially stigmatised and who live in neighbourhoods lacking civil structures. It is this picture of multiple disadvantage that particularly characterises offenders in prison and subject to supervision by the probation service, stigmatised because of their use of drugs, the nature of their offences or their chaotic circumstances or lifestyles.
- Voluntary sector organisations (VSOs) often have specialist knowledge, experience or skills. This is classically the case with those specialising in drug treatment (which often involve former addicts) and prisoner families (usually the outgrowth of personal experience).
- VSOs are often self-help, user or autonomous groups who, because they are generally independent of existing official structures and models, are not so bound by bureaucratic rules and structures (including managerial targets) and are often able, therefore, to deliver services in new, innovative, more flexible ways.
- Because they are less tainted by authority, VSOs are generally more free to be, or be seen to be, on the users' side. The implication is that they are likely to have greater legitimacy with users.

There is of course a paradox here. *The Cross Cutting Review* acknowledged that VSOs are generally highly dependent on state or local state funding. And to the extent that state agencies are hidebound by targets and process rules when dispensing money, then so, to a considerable extent, are VSOs. However, it seemed to me that some influential figures within the probation service entertained other views about volunteers and the voluntary sector which were distinctly questionable or unhelpful:

- That the available pool of volunteer effort is diminishing or has largely been drained and it is no longer worth making the effort of fishing in it.
- That working with volunteers and many voluntary groups is more trouble than it is worth: organising them or working with them is costly and disruptive and the quality of what is provided is often poor.
- The new, highly professionalised NPS can do what is needed better. So why make the effort?

42 Tim Newburn and Michael Shiner, *Young People, Mentoring and Social Exclusion* (Cullompton: Willan Publishing, 2005).

43 Chris Attwood, Gurchand Singh, Duncan Prime and Rebecca Creasey *2001 Home Office Citizenship Survey: people, families and communities;* Home Office Research, Development and Statistics Directorate, London: Home Office, 2003).

The latter views appeared to be most prevalent among the new breed of correctional technicists, many of them within the National Probation Directorate (NPD), developing the promised land of cognitive behavioural offender programmes and electronic surveillance. For them, community engagement was judged 'pre-science' and distinctly 'Old Probation', out of keeping with the emerging preoccupation with offender risk assessment and management, tasks best left to the professionals. All of which makes resuscitation, in the context of NOMS, of the community engagement prospect under *civic renewal* within *offender management* ironic, but no less welcome for that.

My experience with youth justice and the Youth Justice Board since 2004 has reinforced my view that volunteers and the voluntary sector have an enormous contribution to make to the prevention of re-offending. First, it is quite untrue that there are not plenty of volunteers. The reformed youth justice system provides a useful pointer to what can be achieved. There are already some 10,000 volunteers working with the 156 Youth Offending Teams (YOTs) in England and Wales, as members of Youth Offender Referral Panels, as appropriate adults and as mentors.[42] This support army is about the same size as the FTE youth justice professional workforce and, following some initial advertising, is in most parts of the country being expanded and replaced largely on the basis of word-of-mouth recommendation, clear evidence that the work is considered intrinsically rewarding. This should come as no surprise. We know from the Home Office 2001 *Citizenship Survey* that 39 per cent of the population is involved in formal volunteering and 67 per cent in informal volunteering.[43] In 2004 the Youth Justice Board (YJB) commissioned its own survey to assess potential public

44 Tim Newburn et al, *The Introduction of Referral Orders into the Youth Justice System: Final Report,* Home Office Research Study No.242 (London: Home Office, 2002).

interest in voluntary effort with young people who offend. The results showed that an estimated 13 million adults in England and Wales would 'signal some level of interest in volunteering' and on the basis of 8 per cent of respondents, an estimated 3.4 million would be 'very interested'. Of the latter, the largest proportion, an estimated 2.7 million, would be 'very interested' in assisting young people develop their literacy and numeracy skills. The survey also showed, however, that the factor most important in determining whether potential volunteers get engaged is the professional training and support available to them before they start and thereafter. This confirmed YOTs' experience with Referral Panel members.[44] A Youth Justice Board survey of YOTs in December 2002 showed that more training was proving necessary for both volunteers and those youth justice workers who supervise them. Accredited training is particularly important when recruiting young and black and minority ethnic group volunteers a sizeable number of whom see participation as a potential first step in career progression.

Secondly, at the YJB we see the involvement of volunteers and/or voluntary sector partnerships (many of which involve volunteers) as a hugely important promotional opportunity for reasons that go beyond the *Cross Cutting Review* rationale. Investment in this field would:

- broaden recruitment of a more diverse, trained workforce (the Youth Justice National Qualifications Framework is being developed with this in mind)
- increase public understanding of and confidence in the youth justice system
- promote the social inclusion of young offenders
- assist the core of professional youth justice workers in tackling the practical social disadvantages – lack of educational attainment and vocational training skills, housing and health problems, lack of familial support, etc – which most persistent young offenders suffer from a combination of.

The positive turning points in most people's lives stem from relationships characterised by continuity, trust and positive engagement, relationships which inspire and lift the subject's eyes above the horizon, relationships which build motivation and through which a way is found on what often appear to be overwhelming practical and personal problems. That is as true with adults as with young offenders, and this point has repeatedly been made in the probation literature.[45] The 'what works' literature emphasises that if offenders' practical problems are not addressed, then cognitive behavioural offender programmes are not likely to work. The emerging lessons from the youth justice field suggest that good volunteer mentoring schemes can prove invaluable in this context.

The third lesson I take from youth justice is the merit of devolving decision-making regarding contracting out. To illustrate, practically every YOT area now provides a variety of early crime prevention schemes:

- Youth and Inclusion and Support Panels (YISPs), comprising representatives of the key agencies (police, education, health, social services and the YOT) working voluntarily with 8-13 year olds identified as at risk of offending, the aim being to support the young people and their families in accessing mainstream services with a view to addressing the factors in their lives that put them at risk of offending.
- Youth Inclusion Programmes (YIPs) which aim to engage, voluntarily, the 50 young people and their families in an area who the key agencies identify as most at risk of offending, again with the aim of addressing the factors in their lives that place them at risk through positive activities, offending behaviour programmes and improved access to services, particularly education.[46]

To take another example, every YOT now offers an Intensive Supervision and Surveillance Programme (ISSP) to the court for serious, persistent young offenders on the cusp of custody, either as a bail condition, or as part of a community sentence, or following release from a custodial sentence where there is a significant risk of breach of licence and recall.[47] All these initiatives, YISP, YIPs and ISSPs, were initially supported with ring-fenced funding from the YJB. However, both originally and currently – these programmes have now been rolled out across the country – it is left to YOT managers locally to determine whether the various supervisory and other offender services should be provided in-house or contracted out. They do so in the light of

45 Shadd Maruna, *Making Good: How Ex-Convicts Reform and Rebuild Their Lives* (Washington: American Psychological Association, 2002); S. Farrall, *Rethinking What Works with Offenders: Probation, Social Context and Desistance from Crime* (Cullompton: Willan Publishing, 2002).

46 Morgan Harris Burrows, *Evaluation of the Youth Inclusion Programme* (London: Youth Justice Board, 2003).

47 Emily Gray, Emily Taylor, Colin Roberts and Simon Merrington, Fernandez and Moore, *ISSP: The Final Report* (London: Youth Justice Board, 2005).

local circumstances and the availability and quality of voluntary sector providers. Unlike NOMS and the NPS we, the YJB, are unable to say what proportion of total YOT expenditure is absorbed by contracted out services: YOTs are accountable to and managed by the local authorities and this is not information we ask of them. However, we know that a sizeable proportion of YISP, YIP and ISSP schemes are contracted out to voluntary sector organisations, both national and local. Though common standards have to be met and data returned as a condition of the YJB grant, the dominant characteristic from this funding and decision-making arrangement is the strong sense of local ownership and the amount of grass-roots innovation. I attribute the high morale in most youth justice teams to two factors – the devolved decision-making and managerial framework and the diversity of genuine partnership provision. Moving in 2004 from probation to youth justice provided me, frankly, with a stark contrast.

It is beyond the scope of this essay to critically discuss the likely arrangements for the future governance of the probation service, the development of probation trusts, their relationships with Regional Offender Managers (ROMS), except to note the following:

- Though the Carter Report and several Home Office documents have referred in highly positive terms to the youth justice delivery model, the proposed NOMS/Probation structure does not even remotely replicate it. Determining who is to provide services at national or regional level arguably provides neither the account-ability nor sensitivity to local conditions and local state agencies which YOTs embody and which area Probation Boards promise in theory.
- NOMS has yet to state any principles which should govern the proposed market in probation services (this was accomplished for prisons through the provisions in the Criminal Justice Act 1991 for the appointment of a Crown 'controller' in each private-ly managed prison, etc). Are any aspects of probation work – the preparation of court reports, for example – to be exempted from the services for which non-public bodies might contract? And, if not, would non-public agencies, voluntary of commercial, prepar-ing court reports be eligible also to deliver interventions possibly

proposed in those court reports? Within the youth justice field we would unequivocally take the view that such overlaps would embody conflicts of interest: the preparation of court reports is the sole responsibility of YOTs.

48 www.pirr.org.uk/prmenu. htm

49 David Walker, 'Are we backing a Trojan horse?', *The Guardian*, 12 July 2006.

I co-founded and was the founding Chair of CLINKS, an organisation dedicated to facilitating the involvement of the voluntary sector in delivering custody and community-based services to offenders. I am delighted to see that CLINKS is closely involved in the *Partners in Reducing Re-Offending* initiative in London with the aim of developing voluntary sector partnerships with probation.[48] I also note that pending publication and passage of the enabling legislation for the formation of probation trusts, Probation Circular 7/2006 requests Probation Boards to increase their spend on the independent sector to five per cent in financial year 2006-7. These suggest that probation engagement with the voluntary sector is being resuscitated. Yet I have my doubts about the progress that will be made early. Most VSOs are either national or very local – I know of virtually none that are essentially regional – and the future is uncertain. As a consequence I am sceptical that the five per cent spending target for this financial year will be achieved. Quite apart from their short-term resource constraints, are Probation Boards likely enthusiastically to contract out services to VSOs with whom, when Probation Trusts are instituted, they will as trusts presumably then have to compete?

Finally, the emphasis within the probation field on 'contestability' suggests, ironically, that the essence of the case set out for the voluntary sector in the *Treasury Cross-Cutting Review* may be being lost sight of in favour of cost-cutting, general denigration of the public services and the emergence of a VSO general we-can-do-better-than-the-public-sector line of argument, which may make some VSOs indistinguishable from commercial providers.[49] It should not be long before the Charities Commission starts asking questions about the VSOs preparing their bids regionally or nationally to take over probation services. What claim, for example, do they have to representing users' experience or interests or having local knowledge of the practical problems facing ex-prisoners? Encouraging partnerships with VSOs is one thing, dismantling the probation service is another matter entirely. Within the youth justice field we favour building the independent professionalism, corporate identity, pride and influence of YOT managers, not reducing them to cautious ciphers. If offenders are to have the self-confidence to build better lives for themselves they need to work with people who have equivalent confidence in themselves and their agency.

Chapter 7: Supervision in the Community – an alternative approach

By Harry Fletcher

50 Home Office (2004).

Scotland has recently seen the launch of a new national offender management strategy that puts criminal justice onto a completely different path. In the new model, Community Justice Authorities bring together local authorities including the English and Welsh Probation equivalent, the Scottish Prison Service, and key partners, such as the voluntary sector, to produce an integrated approach to reducing re-offending.

   In contrast, on 6th January 2004 the Home Office published, *Reducing Crime – Changing Lives,* an instant response to Patrick Carter's Review of Correctional Services.[50] This created the National Offender Management Service (NOMS), effectively merging the prison and probation services. The two and a half years since the establishment of NOMS have seen a number of different 'visions' emerge for the future of the probation service under the new arrangements, all advocating greater centralisation and regionalisation, coupled with fragmentation of the service, and the introduction of contestability and market forces.

The NOMS Project

The development of the NOMS project has been characterised by a lack of detail, a lack of clarity and a lack of consultation throughout. No business case has been produced on either the creation of NOMS or the introduction of 'contestability'

51 Napo is the trade union, professional association and campaign organisation for more than nine and a half thousand people working in the National Probation Service and the Children and Family Court Advisory and Support Service.

52 Home Office, *Restructuring Probation to Reduce Re-offending*, NOMS Consultation Document (London: Home Office, 2005).

and market forces into the system. Internal risk assessments that have been produced (in October 2004 and March 2005) described the possibility of the project running into difficulties as high and very high.

Time and again Napo,[51] together with many other 'stakeholders', has voiced opposition to each new proposal: to the planned abolition of Probation Boards with their base in local communities; and to the break-up, and effective abolition, of the probation service. It has consistently argued against the introduction of private profit and market forces into the criminal justice system, maintaining they will have a detrimental effect on the Service, on reducing re-offending and on public protection. Throughout the process the government has been consistently losing the argument but nevertheless has seemed determined to push ahead.

Early plans to split the probation service into two separate 'interventions' and 'offender management' sections (effectively a contractor/client split) to simplify opening it up to the private sector were shelved July 2004, following expressions of concern from all quarters about the implications for the service. However, they were soon resurrected, when the then NOMS Chief Executive, Martin Narey, was instructed by the Prime Minister's office to come up with a structure and have it ready for piloting in April 2005. The resulting NOMS Bill was however abandoned in the run up to the May General Election.

The latest consultation document was *Restructuring Probation to Reduce Re-offending,* published in October 2005.[52] In it the Government proposed to abolish the National Probation Service and replace it with a fragmented market of competing providers. Over 70 responses were received, less than 1% of which were in favour of the proposals. Following the Home Office reshuffle in May, the Bill to introduce the restructuring of the Service has been delayed yet again.

The case against privatisation
It is highly controversial that it is being argued that privatisation and market forces will drive up performance when, despite acute resource problems, the probation service is performing better than ever. Figures for November 2005 showed that 'breach' targets were achieved in 92% of cases; 'orders'

were completed in 81% of cases and 'offender behaviour programmes' were completed in 107% of targeted cases. In addition, 8 out of 10 supervisees were still in contact with their probation officer after 6 months of supervision and 93% of victims were contacted within the required period.

Napo believes there is no hard evidence to support the view that contestability will make public sector providers more efficient or less costly to the public. Indeed, the probation service is no stranger to the privatisation agenda and our experience so far leads us to fear the worst.

In 2002 we saw the contracting out of hostel facilities, including cooks, cleaners and maintenance staff with the consequence that costs rose by on average 62%. In 2003, a decision was taken by the NPD to privatise the management and maintenance of probation premises. This in turn led to an immediate increase in costs of 35%. Both privatised projects have been characterised by a fall in service standards.

In 1998 we saw the roll out of curfew orders with electronic tagging operated by private companies who stand to make considerable profits. The cost of electronic surveillance for a full year is £6,500, while the cost of kit (which can be used at least 5 times) is £375, the fitting cost is £150, and the cost of each call out is £150. Evidence collected by Napo, also shows that there are numerous problems with the operation of the tagging and that violations are not routinely monitored.

Napo also believes that the introduction of competition into the provision of community supervision will lead to fragmentation, hostility between agencies that currently co-operate, and it will drive down wages and terms and conditions.

Partnership not competition
Napo believes that there are alternative structures which could deliver the government's aims of public protection, reducing offending and thorough offender management and greater efficiency, through further investment in partnership with the statutory, voluntary and not for profit sectors.

Currently, the probation service is involved in a range of public protection work with the police. This includes multi-agency public protection work where offenders who pose a risk to the public, either through violence or sexual offending,

53 Scottish Parliament, *Community Sentencing – The Tough Option* – A consultation paper (Edinburgh: Scottish Parliament, 1998).

54 Scottish Labour Party, *Scottish Labour's 2003 manifesto – On your side* (Edinburgh: Scottish Labour Party, 2003).

are supervised closely and jointly by the two organisations. In addition, a range of work is carried out, in partnership with the police, with intensive and prolific offenders, particularly those with the problems associated with drugs. The probation service also works with the health services and drug agencies in supervising people on drug treatment orders.

The Service is involved in a range of other partnership work including employment and accommodation. It liaises and works with victim support and alcohol agencies, working in partnership to enhance the possibilities of resettlement. It also provides community service, with a range of other agencies including the youth service, play groups, church and other charitable organisations. Napo believes that all this work, which is widely praised, would be damaged by the introduction of competition at the expense of partnership.

An alternative strategy

In contrast to what is proposed for England and Wales, the Scottish model enhances partnership working and improved co-operation by putting it on a statutory footing.

In Scotland local authorities, often working in conjunction with the voluntary sector, are the main agencies managing community sentences and the rehabilitation of offenders into the community. The 1968 Social Work Act for Scotland gave local authorities what was, in effect, the probation role. In 1998, the Scottish Parliament published a paper *Tough Options,* which looked into the future of the location of criminal justice services within a social work setting.[53] This led to the establishment of regional consortia. There are currently 32 local authorities in Scotland carrying out criminal justice social work. They are now divided into eight criminal justice groupings, plus three Unitary Authorities and the three Island Authorities of Shetland, Orkney and the Western Isles. Consortia have responsibility for delivering social work criminal justice services in boundaries that are roughly co-terminus with the police and sheriffdoms.

A plan for a single corrections agency in Scotland, similar to the one for England and Wales, was published in the Labour Manifesto for the 2003 Scottish Parliament elections.[54] However, after the election, a Labour/Liberal Democrat coalition led to the publication of a consultation paper on reducing re-offending in Scotland.[55] The document asked whether a single agency was the best way forward.

The consultation was widespread, there were 138 written responses, and overwhelmingly the majority of respondents expressed concerns about the establishment of a single agency.

Criticisms included that:

- the agency would not necessarily tackle re-offending
- it would create additional problems and lead to a loss of links at a local level
- it would fail to address the complex range of needs of offenders
- it would reduce the ability to manage risk
- it would involve bureaucracy, disruption and cost, and would divert resources from service provision.

There was a consensus on the shortcomings of the current system, particularly on the need for a more seamless experience for offenders, especially at the transition points between the custodial and the non-custodial parts of the system; the need for better sharing of information between all parties; and the need for better planning. However, Ministers were persuaded by responses to the consultation exercise that there were other ways to address these problems than by a single agency.

The plans for a single agency were dropped, and instead, in December 2004, the Scottish Executive produced: *"Supporting Safer, Stronger Communities: Scotland's Criminal Justice Plan"*.[56] Its main proposals were to:

- introduce a National Advisory Body, chaired by the Minister for Justice to advise on a national strategy for offender management and to ensure a clear, shared focus on reducing re-offending
- legislate to introduce a statutory framework to place the Scottish Prison Service and local authorities under specific new obligations to work closely together to manage offenders seamlessly and to reduce re-offending
- legislate to bring groups of local authorities together in new joint Community Justice Authorities, responsible for ensuring the consistent and effective delivery of criminal justice social work across the area

55 Scottish Executive, *Re:duce, Re:habilitate, Re:form – A consultation on Reducing Reoffending in Scotland* (Edinburgh: Scottish Executive, 2004).

56 Scottish Executive, *Supporting Safer, Stronger Communities: Scotland's Criminal Justice Plan* (Edinburgh: Scottish Executive, 2004).

- require the Scottish Prison Service and the Community Justice Authorities to prepare and deliver an area offender management plan to reduce re-offending;
- legislate to support the work done by the police, criminal justice social work and the Scottish prison service, assisted by a range of other agencies, in assessing and managing the risk from sex offenders and to support better systems for sharing information.

This was followed by the Management of Offenders (Scotland) Act in November 2005. The main clauses of the Act place a duty on the criminal justice agencies in local government to co-ordinate with the Scottish prison service to share information, to prepare and submit annual plans and to involve others in planning the new Community Justice Authorities. It also legislates to allow partners to be consulted on area plans and places a duty on the Community Justice Authorities to establish information sharing networks with partners. The model will be firmly based on partnership rather than market testing, contestability, or privatisation.

The Community Justice Authorities, which will be made up of locally elected councillors, will be required to produce area plans on how this cooperation will be realised, and funding for the Criminal Justice Social Work will in future be channelled through them. Ministers believe that this mechanism will provide for their aim of securing increased national direction in criminal justice social work, whilst maintaining its local delivery.

Creating Change

The Scottish Executive stated in May 2006 that to deliver such a wide range of service improvements required time. Their strategy proposes that services should be developed under five inter-linking themes.

- setting priorities
- working together in new ways
- developing and supporting the workforce
- communication
- measuring, learning and acting.

The Scottish Executive has set itself the vision of stronger, safer communities where ordinary people can live their lives free from the fear of crime and where the rights of all members of the community are respected and upheld. Their current target is a 2% reduction in reconviction rates in all types of sentence by March 2008.[56] The Executive has stated that over the next financial year it will work with a new national advisory body to set targets for 2008 onwards.

In Napo's view, the changes underway in Scotland have been driven by a concern to increase the effectiveness of all services in reducing re-offending, but in England there is a real risk that structural changes based on the creation of a purchaser/provider split and competition will be counterproductive, overly bureaucratic and will not have the impact that the government desires. Indeed, this model is likely to be of greater benefit to the voluntary sector if it leads to fixed long-term contracts, means that bidding capacity will be kept to a minimum and results in partnership on a statutory basis.

56 Scottish Executive, *Reducing Reoffending: National Strategy for the Management of Offenders* (Edinburgh: Scottish Executive, 2006).